I AM ENOUGH

Recovering from Intimate Betrayal

© 2020 Kelly L. Howarth
All rights reserved.
Montreal, Quebec, Canada
InfiniteU Press @ www.infiniteUcoaching.com
Printed in Canada.
ISBN 978-1-7753154-0-7 (Print)
ISBN 978-1-7753154-1-4 (Digital)

It is strictly prohibited to reprint, reproduce, or distribute this book, in part or whole, without the express written consent of the author. Please direct any inquiries to the author at www.infiniteU-coaching.com, Canada.

Cover design by Top Hit Design and Eswari Kamireddy
Cover image by Jenko Ataman
Author image by Walmart Canada
Interior layout by Eswari Kamireddy

Kelly L. Howarth has no responsibility for the persistence or accuracy of URLs for external or third-party Internet websites referred to in this publication and does not guarantee that any content on such websites is, or will remain, accurate or appropriate.

Disclaimer: Any names and likenesses appearing in this book are coincidental—the characters are composites. Other names and story details have been changed or withheld to protect the confidentiality of those individuals who have shared their stories. Any personal events recounted by the author derive from her recollections, which she recalls to the best of her knowledge. We know that memories, like photographs, sometimes fade and blur. The stories are not intended to defame or harm, but instead, aim to help those who've experienced the same. Any suggestions are not intended to replace the help of a qualified therapist or medical doctor.

Acknowledgments

First, I would like to acknowledge Life as my best teacher. Life has brought me all my lessons, thrusting me into a place of readiness to engage with change — a place where I now reside in myself fully and authentically. Life compelled me to face myself finally and learn to trust and love myself unconditionally.

I have profound gratitude for Mary Grace "Bunny" Dorais, my beloved mother. An imaginative storyteller, Mom regaled me with fantastic tales — each one rich with meaning — for our fourteen years together. She inspired me to listen to the stories of others, too, which, as Life would have it, I now do professionally.

Thank you to my child, who has inspired me to be the best version of myself because parenting has helped me grow. You provided me with the opportunity to be a positive role model.

Much gratitude to my dear husband, Luigi; thank you for your late-night edits. Your love and support give me the courage to continue on my path.

Thank you, Patricia Wright, my friend since the age of seven, for your encouragement and support of my journey and for encouraging me to put more of my voice into this book. Pat taught me the principle of allowing into my new life only what I love.

Thank you to my friend and fellow life coach, Andrea Walters, for gently coaching me to write my story with authenticity and heart and for coaching me to the finish line.

Many heartfelt thanks to my friend, Claudia Del Balso, editor, for accompanying and supporting me on my literary journey through our writing partnership, for your discerning edits, and for cheer-leading me each step of the way.

Sincere gratitude to Renata Sielecki, editor and technical writer, for casting your keen editorial eye and suggesting critical developmental edits and image copyright assistance.

Much appreciation and gratitude for my dear friend, Eleanor Cowan, for your writing coaching and mentoring, your patient rereads and edits, and your enthusiastic encouragement to birth this book.

Many thanks to my dear friend, Jane Nicholson, English Second Language Teacher, for her insightful edits to the final manuscript.

Much gratitude to the courageous Julie Dubreuil, a survivor of intimate betrayal, who did a final read and beta-test of *I AM ENOUGH* at a time when she was experiencing significant upheaval and transition in her life. Thank you for your thoughtful, intelligent, and insightful feedback.

Sincere thanks to all the people in the various support groups I attended, where I learned to live one day at a time and one moment at a time. I am forever grateful for those people who've come into my life as quiet examples of integrity. I am thankful to be part of a collective that supports me.

Much gratitude to all those who have shared insights and information toward informing this topic.

For you — the hero of *your* journey.

*Over and over again, you are called to the realm of
adventure, you are called to new horizons.
Each time, there is the same problem: Do I dare?
And then if you do dare, the dangers are there,
and the help also, and the fulfillment or the fiasco.
There's always the possibility of fiasco.
But there's also the possibility of bliss.*

—Joseph Campbell

Table of Contents

Acknowledgments	iii
Foreword	xi
Introduction	xiii
How You Can Use This Workbook	xix
Chapter 1 - How Does Someone Else's Sexual Behavior Affect You?	1
Chapter 2 - The Discovery	21
Exercise 1: Putting My Feelings Into Words	27
Exercise 2: Drawing My Feelings	28
Exercise 3: What I Now See	30
Exercise 4: Family Legacy of Addiction	37
Exercise 5: Rescuing and Enabling	43
Exercise 6: The Impacts of Someone Else's Sexual Behavior	45
Exercise 7: Join a Support Group	51
Chapter 3 - Living the Cycle of Abuse	53
Exercise 8: My Safety Plan	76
Exercise 9: What Feels Abusive?	77
Chapter 4 - Grieving the Loss	79
Exercise 10: My Story	93
Exercise 11: My Resources	95
Chapter 5 - A Holistic Approach to Healing	97
Exercise 12: Adopt a Somatic Practice	100

Exercise 13: Mirror Mirror	101
Exercise 14: Two-Minute Meditation	106
Exercise 15: Learn About Sex Addiction	107
Exercise 16: How I Am Enough	109
Exercise 17: I AM...	109
Exercise 18: Letting Go—Allowing and Trusting	111
Exercise 19: Trusting My Inner Voice	114
Exercise 20: Trusting My Inner Knowing	114
Exercise 21: Adopt a Regular Holistic Healing Practice	120
Chapter 6 - Stopping and Starting	**121**
Exercise 22: My Stopping Work	128
Exercise 23: My Starting Work	129
Chapter 7 - Moving Forward	**131**
Exercise 24: What If...?	132
Exercise 25: If I Weren't Afraid, I Would...	134
Exercise 26: One Single Boundary	140
Exercise 27: Working Through	141
Exercise 28: What I will not Tolerate in an Intimate Relationship	143
Exercise 29: What I Don't Want in an Intimate Partner	143
Exercise 30: What I Want in an Intimate Partner	143
Exercise 31: How I Am Moving Forward	144
Exercise 32: Honest Conversations	150
Exercise 33: Staying	155
Exercise 34: Leaving	159
Exercise 35: What Triggers Me?	163

Exercise 36: My Priorities	169
Exercise 37: What Would I do If...?	169

Chapter 8 - Embracing the Gains — 171
Exercise 38: My Gratitude Journal — 172
Exercise 39: Prioritizing and Getting My Needs Met — 179
Exercise 40: My Plan for Sexual Self-Expression — 180
Exercise 41: Writing a Love Letter to Myself — 180

Chapter 9 - Rewrite Your Story — 183
Exercise 42: Visioning the Next Chapter of My Story — 184
Exercise 43: What I've Learned that's Worth Remembering — 186

Epilogue — 187

Recommended Resources — 191

Bibliography — 193

Foreword

Say it slowly: "I am enough." Say it standing up with your feet firmly planted, "I am enough." Say it softly and gently as you breathe deep and as you live each day of your precious life. Whenever you want, shout it out, *voce magna*, "I AM ENOUGH!"

Stunned by our partners' sexual acting out, caught up in their addictions, we gasp for air as we flounder in our efforts to deal with their deceptive betrayals.

Kelly Howarth skillfully unhooks our tragic entrapment. I say 'our' because Kelly and I became close friends while teaching life skills and communications classes together in the same adult education center. As we shared course materials and chatted about our programs, our children, and Key lime pie recipes, neither of us were able to acknowledge fully that someone else's sex addiction impacted us. Our shocking discoveries had blindsided us. We felt betrayed — shaken to the core.

In this healing workbook, Kelly skillfully accompanies her readers through the stages involved in waking up to the full impact of intimate partner betrayal. Step-by-step, we are invited to consider our blind tolerance of the unacceptable and our muting of a partner's ungovernable compulsions. We examine the social grooming to silence and its toxic consequences. In my case, I lived in a kind of dissociation, an unconscious protective defense, until I was supported to step out of my constant denial and access the care available to me.

Kelly invites the reader to walk alongside Molly as her story of intimate betrayal unfolds. Molly describes her efforts to deal with each new instance of her partner's reprehensible behavior, which was never, ever supposed to happen again. Commenting upon Molly's hard-earned insights, Kelly guides her readers to access the love, support, and resilience also available to them.

Kelly's powerful reminder is clear: We have what it takes. We are, in ourselves, enough.

Kelly Howarth's healing workbook supports her readers so that each one can, in their readiness, proudly proclaim, "I am enough."

—Eleanor Cowan, author of *A History of a Pedophile's Wife: Memoir of a Canadian Teacher and Writer*

Introduction

If you are reading this book, you've probably discovered that your partner has another side, a hidden side that causes them to act out sexually. This compulsive behavior affects your intimate couple relationship. Your feelings may range from denial to anger to sadness. You may feel hopeless. You may find yourself questioning your sanity and self-worth. You have experienced intimate betrayal by the one person you thought you could trust.

When you decide to become a couple, a deep emotional bond begins to form. This bond is the glue that holds you together. There's a sense that your partner is part of your tribe and that they have your back. They love, respect, and protect you as you do them. You expect that you'll be and feel safe and secure with your partner. Instead, you experience intimate betrayal, any act in which your partner engages that threatens your well-being and the well-being of your relationship. It could be lying, cheating, stealing, abusing, neglecting—all elements of sexual acting out and sex addiction.

Intimate betrayal threatens this bond because, according to psychologist Dr. Steven Stosny (2013), it "strikes at the core of our capacity to trust and love ... there's been a violation of the implicit promise that gives us the courage to love in the first place." What's more, according to Stosny, our reaction to intimate betrayal isn't rational because it comes from the reptilian part of the brain: "It often includes the vague feeling that you might die." Our partner's betrayal threatens that super-glue bond because it puts our attachment at risk, which causes us to feel significant distress. Therefore, we are profoundly devastated by the intimate betrayal.

Intimate betrayal hits you hard. It upends your life—either suddenly when you discover the deceit by accident or slowly as you gradually piece the clues together. Either way, this destructive force has lasting, harmful effects. While it may be possible for a relationship to survive as partners strive to heal through recovery, it's not a straightforward route. Many couple relationships do not survive intimate betrayal because trust, once broken, is not readily rebuilt or restored. Like a vase that has shattered, its fragments glued together again, it will never be the same.

I remember my stunned reaction—followed by disbelief and numbness—when I first discovered that my then-partner was sexually acting out. It felt surreal. Everything came rushing at me as my mind tried to piece together years of random incidents—all the clues I'd failed to connect. They now made sense. The pieces suddenly fit together perfectly. However, this wasn't a pretty picture puzzle where placing the last tile completes an idyllic scene.

Through my pain and anguish, I wanted answers. I sought to learn about other peoples' experiences of living with and loving sex addicts—people with whom I could identify and from whom I could learn. How did they cope? What worked for them? How did others find their way back to feeling whole after intimate betrayal?

Ultimately, I desired healing and recovery. I knew that for me, personal healing needed to happen holistically on all levels of body, mind, and self. My recovery involved exploring a range of different approaches: meditation, Reiki, massage, attending a support group for partners of sex addicts, journaling, wellness retreats, and even studying life coaching. It was not so much the timeline that was important, but rather, the process of restoration.

It occurred to me that if I could experience such a profound life transition and leverage what I'd learned about myself through this change, I could help others do the same. My commitment to healing enabled me to integrate all the aspects of my self that had been fragmented by the intimate betrayal, and ultimately, by all my years of dealing with the addictions of significant others.

You can't control your partner's sexual acting out. You can't control their lust or recovery. It is detrimental to you to even try. You can't ever cure your partner's compulsion to engage in any of these acts. You can only change *you*! By changing from within, this is how you heal from intimate betrayal and from living through the chaos caused by your partner's sex addiction and their sexual acting out. This workbook is about taking back *your* power as you prioritize your needs and your life and commit to healing your body, mind, and self.

Some of the relationships marked by sexual addiction do survive when partners mutually decide and become willing to heal through recovery. However, many couples do not survive intimate betrayal intact. This book does not advocate that you leave your relationship. The decision is yours alone. Instead, this book aims to help you put your healing first. This workbook format provides tools and enables personal reflection. Healing from the hurt is necessary for you to move past the betrayal and learn to trust again—whether you decide to stay or leave.

Why this workbook, *I AM ENOUGH*?

Much writing exists about addiction as a disease characterized by a failure of 'enoughness,' meaning that the addict's cycle of addictive behavior is triggered because they don't feel they are good enough. We, as the partners of sex addicts, often question whether we are enough when faced with their compulsive behavior. When someone intimately betrays us, we are vulnerable to terrible feelings of inadequacy and emptiness. We experience a deep hurt. We feel robbed of the confidence that connects us to our sense of 'enoughness.' So, the healing must go deep for us to find our way back to feeling good about ourselves and trusting that we are enough. We must learn to love and value ourselves *exactly as we are*.

This workbook forms a blueprint for healing. The stories and activities presented here were born out of my own need to heal from the devastating impacts of a relationship with a sex-addicted partner and to break the lifelong cycle of abuse inflicted by all the addicts in my life.

This workbook is for you, whether you're male, female, or self-described (gender-neutral, binary, etc.), and regardless of your sexual orientation. It doesn't matter what belief systems you may or may not hold. The number of months or years you've invested in your relationship isn't relevant. It doesn't amplify or lessen the agony. Intimate betrayal is crushing!

The exercises in this workbook will help you explore your inner world. They will enable you to dig deep. They will assist you to come to terms with the effects of intimacy with a partner whose sexual acting out is an outright betrayal—of your trust, of your values, of your boundaries, and your dreams for your life together as a couple (and family).

You are invited to journey with Molly through her story of intimate betrayal by Kevin, her sex-addicted partner. Molly's narrative starts with her vague awareness that something is not quite right. It then moves to her sudden discovery of her partner's sexual acting out and progresses through her self-help trajectory, providing insights she acquired along the way. You'll also read other brief accounts that parallel Molly's story and corroborate the impacts.

These narratives intend to shine a bright light on addiction and abuse. They highlight how a partner's addiction keeps us shackled. Hopefully, the stories here serve to light the path away from despair and darkness.

I encourage you to treat the individual stories and exercises in this book as firm railings you can grasp to steady yourself on your climb back into your richly deserved happiness.

How You Can Use This Workbook

Get a notebook or journal to use as you explore these exercises. Note the date at the top of the page, along with the activity and page number so that you can refer to these as needed. You may choose to progress through this book chapter by chapter or explore the sections randomly. There is no prescribed order. However, take some time to pause and reflect. Meditate or play relaxing music in the background. Do what you need to do to create your very own safe space.

Resist the temptation to merely read the exercises without doing them, to hurry through them, or to only go partway through completing them. Why? Because immersing yourself in the challenging work of healing from the impact of your partner's sex addiction will help you grow stronger and recover from the trauma you've experienced. You've taken the

> " Be the change you want to see in your world.

fundamental first step of acquiring this book. You must now do the heavy lifting—the real work of helping yourself heal.

Healing is a complicated process that doesn't always happen in a straight line. But it's well worth the journey. Your commitment to healing from intimate betrayal is the most significant, most decisive step you can take to empower yourself. Be the change you want to see in your world. *You are worth it!*

Chapter 1

How Does Someone Else's Sexual Behavior Affect You?

Molly's partner, Kevin, regularly consumed alcohol and pot. He also had a long-standing habit of viewing porn on the television and the Internet. Molly noticed that Kevin gawked at women when they were in public together. Then, one day, she discovered Kevin was invasively peeping at women in their private spaces. Molly confronted Kevin, and her life changed.

***

Oliver wondered why Megan's computer had held her rapt attention over the past few months. When she left her monitor to take a phone call, Oliver looked at the screen. On it was a sex chat!

***

Linda couldn't quite place the charges on the statement of the credit card she shared with her partner: charges for hotels, long-distance calls, and expensive restaurants. When she asked Robert, he said they were work-related expenses, which his employer would reimburse. Linda had never seen an expense claim check going through their joint bank account. She eventually learned that Robert was having sexual affairs with women she considered her friends.

***

Mandy regularly met with friends. Gill, her husband, was cool with that until these meetings became more frequent and occurred without explanation. Gill noticed Mandy's gradual emotional withdrawal from their relationship. He couldn't understand her aloofness but sensed she was hiding something. He soon learned that Mandy was continually starting new infatuations with the men she met online and in bars.

***

Ken, who was in a long-term relationship with Jules, learned that his partner had been frequenting adult bookstores and bathhouses, hanging out in parks late at night, and meeting strangers for sex in the shadows. He discovered this after confronting Jules when his own HIV test came back positive.

***

Jessica found herself at the local police station for the second time in three months, posting bail for her husband, Andrew, who had again been caught showing himself naked to a group of teenage girls walking home from school.

***

Gabriel didn't understand it: his wife withheld sex for weeks, sometimes months at a time. Then there'd be binges where they'd have plenty of sex in short bursts before another dry spell began.

***

Margie was stunned and confused when crime-unit police showed up with a search warrant at the home she shared with her children and new husband, Richard. Without explanation, the officers removed computers and cell phones. Margie learned that the beloved partner she thought she knew so well was distributing online child pornography.

***

Lorna was astounded to learn that she and her husband, Stan, would lose their home. How could this be? After all, he ran a successful business. Lorna soon discovered that Stan had been paying for prostitutes with company funds and had run through their entire joint savings.

***

Marion was proud of the beautiful home and privileged lifestyle she enjoyed with her husband, William, yet she felt so alone because he traveled two weeks a month. After twenty-three years of marriage, Marion discovered that William had been leading a double life: he had another family with another woman fifteen years his junior!

***

Millions of supporters worldwide joined the 2017 #MeToo Movement, sharing their stories of the sexual harassment and abuse they had suffered at the hands of public figures, family members, and private citizens. The perpetrators of the victims in the #MeToo

Movement likely have partners and caring families who have been shocked to learn that their loved ones are sex abusers.

***

All the people presented in these scenarios share the collective experience of intimate betrayal because of a partner's compulsive sexual behavior. Their trust and faith in their partner and their couple relationship—and even in themselves—has been shattered.

What is Addiction?

Imagine visiting Utopia—a place where you can have anything you want anytime you want. You feel good in this dreamland because it lets you escape your pain. Except you're only a visitor to this perfect place and don't live there. You soon find yourself visiting Utopia more often and lingering longer. You don't want to leave. When you do tear yourself away, you long to return. Your pain becomes too high. It now feels impossible for you to respond to your previous life. You yearn for Utopia.

Addiction is like Utopia. The word addiction describes the condition of being dependent on a substance, thing, or activity. It also includes any pursuit that:

- Involves highly compulsive behavior (mental obsession, always thinking about the source of the addiction).
- Alters the brain chemistry of the individual so that they cannot stop by sheer willpower alone.
- Consumes the addict; they become preoccupied with the substance.
- Progresses (often gets worse).

- Leads to losses: health, job, legal, marital, mental, social, and financial.
- Can involve dependency on multiple substances, things, or activities simultaneously (e.g., using drugs or alcohol and sexually acting out).
- Presents the addict as living in contradictions—they tell you that they love you, yet they act out sexually, often with others.
- Involves engaging in sexual behavior about which the addict feels ashamed or sad.
- Involves the addict promising themselves and others that they will stop the behavior or never sexually act out again.

When considering addiction, we usually think of alcohol and drugs. Sex, too, is a substance on which one can be dependent. The problem is that sex is a sensate substance. Like food, it appeals to every sense: vision, hearing, taste, smell, and touch. Coupled with the initial void the addict seeks to fill, the tremendously pleasurable feelings associated with sex make controlling the compulsion especially tricky for the sex addict. The sex addict may have tried treatment (to leave Utopia) that wasn't successful in arresting their compulsive sexual behavior.

Sex addiction is almost as prevalent as cardiovascular disease, affecting an estimated three to six percent of adults. And sex addiction occurs in people of all socio-economic and educational levels, ethnicities, and races. Let's look at what sexually compulsive behaviors comprise sex addiction:

- Viewing pornography (sexual images) in all forms
- Listening to audio sex

- Sex chat over the phone or online (cybersex)
- Extramarital affairs and one-night stands
- Incest or sex with a family member
- Deviant sexual acts (paraphilic or abnormal, also known as sexual perversions), including:
  - Pedophilia—sexual attraction to and sex with children
  - Necrophilia—sexual arousal from and sex with a corpse
  - Somnophilia—sexual arousal from and sex with a sleeping or unconscious person
  - Exhibitionism—exposing themselves naked to others
  - Frotteurism/groping—sexually bumping, rubbing up against, or touching someone without their consent
  - Voyeurism—'Peeping Tom' activities (peering in windows or observing others through binoculars)
  - Zoophilia or bestiality—sex with animals
  - Sexual sadism (sexual arousal from inflicting pain on another)
  - Sexual masochism (sexual arousal from inflicting pain on oneself)
  - Transvestism—dressing in opposite-sex clothing for arousal
  - Fetishism—sexual arousal or gratification linked to an object, part of the body, or item of clothing
- 'Upskirting'—taking pictures up an unsuspecting individual's skirt or taking sexual photographs of anyone without their knowledge or consent

- Sexual acts with random strangers in adult bookstores, in parks, in the shadows, etc.
- Paying for sex with prostitutes or engaging with escorts
- Flirting with others to get sex
- Multiple sexual relationships
- Continually talking about sex in everyday conversations
- Hypersexuality - dysfunctional preoccupation with sexual fantasy (can combine with any of the others listed here)
- Infatuations and emotional connections with others (love addiction)
- Always wanting to have sex with you, pressuring you for more sex than you want or like, and not respecting your 'No.'
- Rarely wanting to have sex with you, withholding sex, or withdrawing emotionally
- Sexually objectifying you (or others)
- Masturbating compulsively as part of any or all the above acts
- Any other act that causes feelings of sexual degradation, humiliation, or discomfort for you as a partner

Your partner may compulsively and consistently engage in one or more of these behaviors and may lie to cover up their actions.

Any diagnosis of sex addiction is based on these warning signs:

1. Sexual desires take precedence over all other responsibilities and needs.
2. Sex is used as a salve for emotional reactions (both positive and negative).

3. Compulsive sexual behavior, such as masturbating, along with the inability to stop thinking about sex.
4. Compulsive use of pornography.
5. Compulsive seeking out of illicit activity to fulfill sexual urges, i.e., pornography, prostitution, sexual harassment/abuse, and rape or thoughts of rape.

First, know this: someone else's choice to compulsively act out sexually is not your fault. You didn't cause it. You can't control it. And you can't cure it (Al-Anon, *Courage to Change*, 1992). You certainly did not drive your partner to engage in any of the compulsive sexual behaviors listed above.

Eminent sex addiction researcher Dr. Patrick Carnes proposes that the sex addict enters a cycle of addiction, a continuous circular pattern of sexual behavior with distinct markers. Here is a depiction adapted from Dr. Carnes' six-stage cycle of addiction:

The Cycle of Addiction

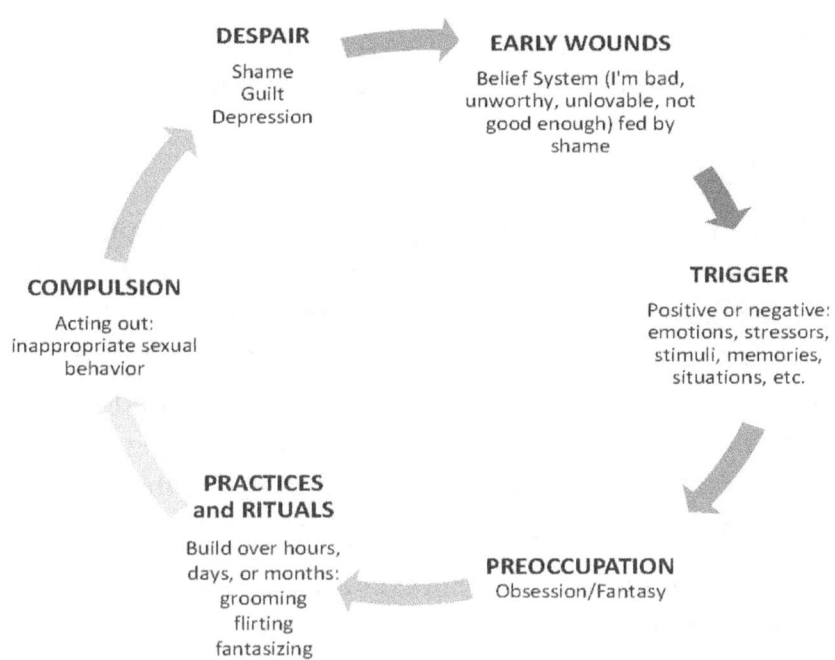

Figure 1: Adaptation of Dr. Patrick Carnes' Cycle of Addiction

This cycle begins with early childhood wounds and an unhealthy belief system resulting from hurts inflicted by significant childhood relationships, such as physical, sexual, or emotional abuse and neglect. It progresses through the various stages of being triggered, meaning that an event or situation gives rise to certain feelings that make the sex addict want to fill a void or salve their unresolved emotional pain. They then engage in rituals, such as any behavior that might lead up to committing the sexually compulsive act. An example is going to a club and flirting as a precursor to becoming aroused and then picking up a stranger for sex (the actual sexual acting out). The result is despair, leading to the shame and guilt of sexually acting out. Then the cycle begins all over again.

What started as an impulse that leads to sexual behavior turns into a compulsion when used habitually to salve pain or stress.

Ruth's Story

Ruth's husband, Connor, displays some of the typical characteristics of a sex addict. He feels unloved. Connor's uncle molested him when he was a prepubescent child. He'd never told his parents so that they couldn't protect him from the continuing abuse. The molestation only stopped when Connor was in his mid-teens, and his uncle died. If we look at Connor while considering the cycle of addiction, we see a sex addict, wounded from childhood emotional, physical, and sexual abuse and neglect.

During his formative childhood years, Connor developed certain core beliefs about himself of which he was not aware—beliefs about being evil and unworthy. He felt shameful and unlovable. Feelings of abandonment, compounded by disbelief that anyone could ever meet his needs, led to Connor's sense that sex was the only way to feel loved. If they are believers, some of the people in Connor's situation may even think that God has abandoned them.

Ruth expressed her observation that Connor seemed to be on a never-ending quest for love and affection that couldn't be satisfied through sex with her—no matter how frequently they engaged in it. While sex addicts may do a lot of touching, none of it qualifies as intimacy. So, they remain untouchable or unreachable in their hearts. Ruth explained that she couldn't emotionally connect with Connor. Because sex addicts never feel satisfied, they cannot fill their void.

Ruth named Connor's behavior deceptive, both of himself and her. He seemed convinced that he didn't have a problem controlling his sexual compulsions, especially when Ruth discovered that he had been trolling the Internet for one-night stands. When she confronted him, Connor pleaded with Ruth. He promised her he'd stop, but the secrets persisted. It became clear that Connor was leading a double life — one that fit society's norms and expectations and presented a picture of himself as happy with his wife and children. His other life had Connor feeding his addiction with multiple affairs. Despite the guilt and shame, despite Ruth's pleading, and despite Connor's many promises, Connor would not get help. Today, Ruth continues to share a living space with him, but nothing else, as she distances herself from Connor and considers her next steps.

***

Joel's Story

Another example of the cycle of addiction is Joel's sexual acting out. Joel feels increasingly stressed by his job. The stress triggers him because it reminds him of the void he feels. He arrives home Friday night after a particularly grueling week and finds the house empty. His wife is working late. The kids are out with friends.

Joel flicks on the large-screen television that's hooked up to the Internet and surfs porn — the ritual of Joel's sexual acting out. The room immediately fills with moans of sex and lust. Joel gets turned on. He recalls all the other times he has felt this deep void and how his go-to friend, Marsha, has been available for him. Joel calls her cell phone. No answer. He suddenly remembers Nicky and quickly punches in the digits. She picks up, welcoming him over. He's out the door in a flash, passing his wife, Lisa, on the way: "Gotta go back to the office—something has come up." She gives him a quizzical look and tells him she'll order dinner for them. Joel knows better than to tell Lisa he won't be home to eat together. His feelings of guilt are assuaged by his anticipation of arriving at Nicky's door and the lust-fest to follow.

***

The accompanying feelings at each stage of the cycle fuel the addict's compulsive behavior (visits to Utopia). The addict sexually acts out to self-soothe underlying feelings of fear, shame, and sadness, and to avoid unresolved inner pain. Reminder: You can never, ever fix this problem because it resides with the addict.

Even though the sexual acting out causes severe problems in their lives, sex addicts often feel powerless to stop themselves. An article in *Newsweek* explains: "Substance abusers and sex addicts alike form a dependency on the brain's pleasure-center neurotransmitter, dopamine. It's all about chasing that emotional high" (Lee, 2011).

Steve's Story

Steve wanted to leave his sex-addicted wife, Julie. He'd find himself desperately tracking Julie to their local pub where she'd be sitting at the bar, hanging off a man, yet again. Steve suspected that Julie was a love addict—looking for love and attention through sex. The fallout from his wife's behavior was impossible to avoid. They lived in a small town where rumors circulated quickly. Men would regularly approach Steve and complain about Julie's fickleness. Steve finally left Julie but returned less than a year later amid promises that things would be different this time. After a few short months, a distraught Steve conveyed his despair that Julie was again sexually acting out.

***

Connor, Joel, and Julie are chasing an emotional high, not unlike that produced by other substances such as alcohol or drugs. Dopamine is the brain chemical responsible for that high. And it takes more and more for the addict to get those feelings of pleasure from engaging in their compulsive behavior. Many addicts report feeling numbed out. Someone once told me: "I'm trying to feel something," referring to their quest for that adrenaline rush. In the case of the sex addict, their behavior becomes reckless. They destroy their relationships with their partners and families, lose jobs, get sexually transmitted diseases, go broke after using their financial resources to pay for sexual services, and often end up in trouble with the law because their sexual acting out crosses over into criminal behavior. Unfortunately, some sex addicts even lose their lives (by engaging in risky sexual practices, neglecting their mental and physical health, putting themselves in dangerous situations involving other people, committing suicide, etc.).

Julie Gruenbaum-Fax's article summarizes the sex addict's reality:

> *But addicts say there is no pleasure in being a slave to a compulsion so strong that it affects the body and mind as acutely as a drug.*
>
> *"There is still this judgment of 'what a sleazy guy,' but what they don't understand is that the addict has a psycho-biological disorder in which he is seeking a drug that he himself produces," said Robert Weiss, clinical director of the Sexual Recovery Institute, on Olympic Boulevard, just outside Beverly Hills. "He is literally dosing himself with his own neurochemistry, like a drug addict with a needle in his arm."*

> *Whether acting out by compulsively masturbating to pornography, having serial affairs, frequenting prostitutes or habitually seeking homosexual or heterosexual one-night stands, sex addicts sink into a pit of shame and self-loathing, often threatening their families and livelihood. (The Jewish Journal,* March 6, 2003, online)

As with any addiction, the severe consequences associated with sexual acting out result in a downward spiral. According to Patrick Carnes, addiction is a brain disease that ultimately affects the addict's perceptions. Dr. Robert A. Moran echoes this: "The disease of addiction has advanced to the point where it has hijacked the brain. The person will now do whatever it takes to seek out and obtain the substance, regardless of the consequences" *(LoveFraud,* July 13, 2018).

We have great difficulty wrapping our minds around addiction as a disease. We think of disease as an illness, like cancer, that someone gets and how its spread is beyond their control. We might think: *Getting a disease is something that happens to us, but the addict chooses to use that substance. It's a choice!* The point here is not to make any pronouncements about sex addiction as a disease, but rather, to illustrate how someone else's compulsive sexual behavior affects us.

Just as we feel powerless to change the sex addict and their acting out, they feel powerless to stop their sexually compulsive behavior. Until the sex addict becomes truly self-aware and actively chooses (and keeps choosing) treatment and recovery, the sexual acting out keeps happening, the risks escalate and intensify, and the cycle continues. As partners, we get swept into the cycle.

Multiple Substances, Multiple Addictions

It's common for an addict to engage in various addictions simultaneously. The statistic is that 83 percent of self-identifying sex addicts are dependent on another substance.

Here's how it rolls: A multiply addicted partner may drink alcohol, which removes constraints and spurs them to enter the second addiction. Now, with their inhibitions dissolved, they flirt more easily and pursue sex more readily. Use of each substance paves the way for engaging in the next behavior. Commingling various substances creates a complex, layered web of addiction.

***

Oren's Story

Oren claims it's far easier for him to identify as an alcoholic, especially considering his marriage. There's less stigma attached, and he gets to hide behind his drinking. Without wine, the flirting, which leads to sexual acting out behavior, is forestalled. When he drinks, however, Oren admits he enters a world of loosened inhibitions. As he recounts, "All bets are off. I find myself playing the game of flirting, which goes further and further. Then I wake up the next morning in someone else's bed, wondering what the hell I've done." He crawls back home to his disheartened wife, who believes his story of passing out at a drinking buddy's house.

***

Molly's Journey

Molly and Kevin were both professionals in their early forties when Molly first discovered Kevin's sex addiction. Molly is a soft-spoken, articulate woman. She claims her ex-partner, Kevin, is smart, funny, and charming. He is driven—yet often unfocused. "When I started dating Kevin, he was trying to quit cigarette smoking. He'd told me that he had an addictive personality. Somehow I didn't register this pertinent information, a red flag reported by the addict himself!" Molly said. In Molly's experience, Kevin regularly used substances, including alcohol and marijuana. Using drugs helped lower Kevin's inhibitions: "Kevin would get high and then peep into windows," Molly said.

There are two drivers to sex addiction:

1. **Power** - fuels the sex addict's feeling of control over someone else when acting out sexually.
2. **Sex itself** - renders the sex addict powerless over their compulsive sexual behavior.

Are sex addicts compelled by the power they wield—or are they tied to the addiction because it fills the void? Might power be yet another addictive substance that, paired with sexual compulsion, fuels the sex addiction?

Both power and sex are substances the sex addict uses to salve pain/fill the void, however temporary. Interestingly, while the sex addict feels powerless over their compulsion to act out sexually, part of the high they get derives from the power of controlling the situation and manipulating the people involved (the target of their sexual acting out, their betrayed partner, and possibly others). These two contradicting realities—power and powerlessness—usually net the same result: feelings of shame in the sex addict.

Somnophilia and voyeurism appear to be power-brokering sex addictions because the addict is in charge and in control of another person who is virtually helpless because they are either unconscious or unaware. Alternately, masturbating to pornography looks like an addiction to fill a void. The degrees of power appear to differentiate the behaviors. Remember that addiction is progressive. The sex addiction can escalate from viewing pornography on a screen (relatively harmless but addictive when done compulsively), to peeping into the windows of real people (control over someone unaware), to drugging someone unconscious and raping them (exerting power and control over someone helpless).

Dr. Gabor Mate, the renowned Canadian addiction and trauma expert, explains: "Addiction to power is always about the emptiness that you try to fill from the outside" (2018).

This commingling of substance addictions with behavioral addictions makes the sex addict's recovery tricky. How do you determine which compulsion leads to the other? Which of the dependencies is an addiction? It can be challenging to recover from one addiction without treating the other(s) simultaneously. Sex addicts seeking treatment for sexual compulsion have less chance of success if they are still using alcohol or other mood-altering drugs.

> How to know if you are dealing with someone's compulsive or addictive behavior is by recognizing that the chaos caused by that behavior is affecting you in a profoundly adverse way.

Can we blame the Internet for its abundance of vibrant sexual images and other materials (text, audio, and chat)? The Internet does provide easy access to sex. Online pornography is always expanding, according to surveys, and accounts for 30 percent of all Internet traffic within a growing $97 billion global industry of adult entertainment, which also includes film (Brownstein, 2018). According to *The Ranch*, the recorded amount of time spent on a single porn website in 2016 was equivalent to 5,245 centuries (online, 2018)!

The Internet and other available media (magazines, videos, etc.) do not cause sex addiction. The most significant challenge for most sex addicts is to be able to live in our highly sexualized society and be willing to go to those deep dark places within themselves to heal and recover. The sex addict must decide to take responsibility for their own choices and actions.

Someone's sex addiction is best diagnosed by a qualified professional. How to know if you are dealing with someone's compulsive or addictive behavior is by recognizing that the chaos caused by that behavior is affecting you in a profoundly adverse way. If you are in a relationship with an addict, their deception can challenge your sense of identity to the point that you question yourself.

 Like tricksters or magicians, intimate betrayers are master manipulators.

Like tricksters or magicians, intimate betrayers are master manipulators. They show you a false, skewed, and demeaning picture of what they want you to see. In this cunning way, they divert your attention from their addiction to whatever they want you to believe is wrong with you. It becomes difficult to know what is real. If you are at all vulnerable to being manipulated because of your low self-esteem, then you may be ripe for continued entrapment in the trickery of intimate betrayal.

By reading this book, you're taking control of you and how you react to your situation. You are starting to prioritize your life. That's a huge first step to changing the dynamic of your relationship with the sex addict and ultimately, changing your relationship with yourself.

Chapter 2

The Discovery

You discover that your partner has been sexually acting out and leading a dual life. You are shocked—knocked off your feet! You feel sucker-punched and blindsided. Your reaction may include any or all the following:

- You're asking yourself, "What just happened?"
- You feel enraged.
- You feel deceived and betrayed.
- You can't believe that the situation is even possible.
- You're wondering, "Did my partner go crazy or have a mental breakdown?"
- You're asking yourself, "How could my partner do something so destructive to our family and me?"

Let's look at what matters most here.

Society grooms us. Our family of origin grooms us. Primed to please people, when facing someone's bad behavior, we may sometimes accommodate rather than challenge and confront them about the clues of that behavior. How dare we put up a fuss? We've been socialized to mute, to diminish, and to make everything appear nicey-nicey. Our reactive words express our shock. You may have your own chosen words to express your feelings. Or you may be stunned into utter silence. We each have our massive reaction to the discovery that our intimate partner is sexually acting out.

Lisa's Story

In the scenario above, Joel's wife, Lisa, turned around and got into her car just as Joel was leaving their driveway. It was dark; she didn't think he'd seen her. Lisa slowly tailed Joel as he took a side street that led away from his office. Although she wasn't sure of herself, she was sure of one thing: Joel wasn't going back to his office. She'd heard this excuse enough. It was time to test out her suspicions.

After a few short blocks, Joel stopped at a small house and was greeted at the door by a lithe red-haired woman. Lisa waited from a safe parked distance.

> **❝** We've been socialized to mute, to diminish, and to make everything appear nicey-nicey.

Ten minutes later, she let herself into the unlocked front door to find her naked husband in this woman's bed. Lisa's shock was nothing compared with that of Joel. Lisa had caught Joel in a lie. She saw through his common ruse about having to return to the office. She now knew about Joel's double life.

***

Molly's Journey Continues

Molly's personal story of intimate betrayal had been simmering for a long time. She tolerated many nights alone in bed while Kevin drank wine and watched porn. *But don't all men watch porn?* She justified his behavior to herself, unaware that vast numbers of men shun such low-life activity. Feelings of inadequacy set in: "I couldn't measure up to the two-dimensional pixilated characters he was watching who were younger, slimmer, and more enticing."

Molly began to view herself as unattractive and undesirable, especially after giving birth to her daughter, a life event that brought body and self-image challenges. Sexual intimacy with Kevin dwindled to once a month and often less. Molly questioned her desirability even more because she didn't understand why, as a healthy young couple, she and Kevin weren't having sex.

Over time, Kevin's porn watching turned into unrestrained all-day indulgence, a steadily degrading disturbance to Molly. In their shared office at home, the sexual moaning and panting sounds from his computer did not escape her ears. "Shockingly, I tolerated this gross behavior happening within earshot!" recounted Molly. Grocery shopping together had turned into a tormenting, drawn-out endurance test, as Molly would often find Kevin pretending to be reading product labels while leering at young women shopping in the same aisle. Driving with Kevin through the local private school district at dismissal time was an ogle-fest of young girls dressed in their school uniforms.

As Kevin's compulsion escalated from viewing pornography to gawking at women in public, Molly would complain, plead, bargain, and threaten—to no avail. "Kevin's nonstop staring at young women felt unsettling to me because it was sending a direct message that I wasn't good enough, not beautiful enough, and just not enough," Molly explained how she thought there was something wrong with her. Frequently put down for the way she looked, the way she dressed, and what she did or didn't do, Molly also began to blame herself.

Kevin's verbal assaults diverted Molly's attention from his sexual acting out, causing her to feel unworthy. Kevin's strategy was effective. Just as intended, Molly was distracted away from his sex addiction. She continued to blame herself, and this further eroded her self-esteem: "I felt undeserving and unloved in a relationship I had once trusted." She told herself things would get better. After all, Kevin was the father of their child, a teenage daughter. Molly still did not see the betrayal: "If only I were enough, then none of this would be happening!"

One summer afternoon, Molly made a heartrending discovery: a pair of binoculars, which she'd seen on the patio table just the week before (whose real purpose she hadn't clued in to), now hid beneath a pile of outdoor gear under the back deck. Kevin tried to divert Molly's attention away from this area of the house while they were doing a chore together outside. Of course, Molly looked and found them. Somehow it clicked. She got it: binoculars, Kevin continually going out at night for extended periods, and a deck chair strategically placed in the direct line of sight of the uncovered back window of their downstairs tenant's living room. Molly learned later that their young female tenant had a habit of watching television in the nude during the worst heat of summer that year.

Molly recounted her initial shocking discovery of Kevin's sex addiction: "I was livid! I didn't mince words when I confronted Kevin about his voyeurism after finding the binoculars: 'What the fuck are you looking at?' He explained that he'd been viewing wildlife. 'In a suburban backyard? Really?' I'd found his excuse lame. Kevin finally admitted it and swiftly issued blame: 'Well, she should have put up blinds!'"

Without hesitation, Kevin's first response was to denounce the unsuspecting victim of his ogling. It was all her fault. She should have taken responsibility for installing window covers. Kevin interpreted their tenant's failure to block her windows as an explicit invitation. She was entirely to blame.

Molly paid a visit to the tenant and asked her to put up blinds, telling her that her daughter and friends used the backyard for gatherings—and it would be best for her privacy. "It was only a few weeks later that the tenant moved back to her hometown despite her job being a block away," Molly recounted. "I couldn't tell her that Kevin was peeping in her window! I was covering up, I know, but how could I tell her that?"

Molly explained how she made the connection: "My consciousness flooded with an understanding that until that moment had eluded me!" Only a few years earlier, Molly had found Kevin walking back and forth between two windows at the rear of their home. He'd angled to get a better view through gaps in the back hedge outside and was observing the teenage girl in the adjacent yard, frolicking in the swimming pool with her boyfriend. Kevin told Molly the two teens were having sex. Molly hadn't given it much thought as she left him watching the scene. Somehow, it didn't occur to Molly that such viewing was invasive. She returned to work on her computer.

Molly recalled other clues that hadn't struck her as extraordinary: "On another occasion, Kevin had commented about the next-door neighbor's adolescent son smoking outside their back door with his girlfriend. At the time, I hadn't been curious enough to piece together what he was doing. But the fact that Kevin observed the couple from a long stretch of yard separated by a hedge between both homes told me that he'd used an invasive viewing technique. It all clicked!"

Kevin's consumption of pornography from the television and computer was increasingly repulsive to Molly: "I didn't accept it—not one bit—but learning that Kevin had crept around in the dark with the intent to violate a woman's private space for his jollies was hard-hitting. I finally got it. I was living with a sex addict!"

What's more, Molly found out that this type of sex addiction, called voyeurism, classifies as a legal offense, adding a Kafkaesque dimension to her discovery. Kevin's habits and their associated illicit behaviors finally got her attention: "My blinders were off!" she said.

At that point, Molly had participated for a year in a support group where the insights shared by members helped her have that light-bulb moment and to connect the dots: "I heard so many stories, and while the details differed from my own, the themes of abuse were the same. I finally woke up to the reality that Kevin's sex addiction had steeped my life in chaos for many years. His obsession—commingled with his use of alcohol, marijuana, and nasty verbal put-downs—echoed my childhood with a father who was abusive and continuously drank."

Growing up in the family dynamic of having a chronically ill mother—a fragile woman who had been submissive to a violent, alcoholic, allegedly sex-addicted father—had laid the early groundwork for Molly never feeling good enough.

"Up to that point in our relationship," Molly explained, "I thought I'd been dealing only with Kevin's substance addictions. I believed that once again, I'd found myself in a family relationship with a problem drinker. I had no idea there was so much more. I had been handling the drinking and drug use, telling myself: *It's not as bad as my father who drank regularly and was violent. One day, Kevin will come to his senses."* Still, something continued to aggravate Molly. A piece of the puzzle was missing. Something didn't quite add up for her.

"Learning about Kevin's sexual acting out utterly blindsided me. Getting wise to Kevin's sex addiction was a game changer!" recounted Molly. "I had been blaming only myself. I felt powerless to change the chaos I'd endured and tolerated for many years. At last, I knew. For the first breathtaking time, I knew: This isn't my fault. I no longer felt safe. That very night, I moved into the guest room to get some distance from Kevin and figure things out."

Molly recognized this discovery as her catalyst to make a significant life change: "Despite feeling devastated, I was finally ready!"

EXERCISE 1: PUTTING MY FEELINGS INTO WORDS

Explain the circumstances of first discovering your partner's sexual acting out:

1. How did you first realize your partner's sex addiction?
2. What were your initial reactions?

Write about how you initially felt and what you said or did when you found out.

Sometimes it can be helpful to express ourselves through nonverbal routes like drawing, illustrating, or painting, especially when we're not completely clear on how to say what we're feeling. You can explore using images, lines, squiggles, symbols, splashes of color, or any other freehand method you choose.

Exercise 2: Drawing My Feelings

Draw a picture of how you feel.

Drawing skills are not the point here. Make this as sad, as angry, or as mean-spirited as you like. It can be detailed or simple. The idea is to depict your feelings about your partner's sexual acting out.

As you begin to fit together the pieces of the sex addiction puzzle, you'll notice behaviors that you may have previously missed. Again, this is not your fault. You may be tempted to come down hard on yourself. Instead, credit yourself with becoming aware that your intimate partner's recurring behaviors are part of sex addiction. These include:

- Making promises over and over that they repeatedly break. These could be promises about stopping their sexually compulsive behavior or promises to spend more time with you and your children.

- Lying to you so that you question your reality and perception of that reality. These can be lies of omission or outright lies about their whereabouts, unaccounted-for time, money spent, and others.

- Manipulating you so that you feel you are the one with the problem, that it's all in your head, and that you're imagining things or projecting your feelings onto them.

- Stealing shared resources—time and money—from both your relationship and your family. You don't know how much money you have, where it's kept, and how it's spent.

- Blaming you for their unreasonable and unacceptable behavior, perhaps telling you things like: "If only you had done …," and "If you were more like …," etc.

- Cheating you by leading a carefully hidden double life. Your partner has engineered a dysfunctional relationship with you and your children as they sought sexual gratification from outside sources.

- Criticizing you for your:
    - ❏ Parenting
    - ❏ Spending
    - ❏ Cooking
    - ❏ Appearance/dress
    - ❏ Activities/hobbies
    - ❏ Family and friends
    - ❏ Character
    - ❏ Eating habits
    - ❏ Size/Weight
    - ❏ Choices
    - ❏ Job/career or absence of
    - ❏ House/yard work

❏ Sexual activity, availability, and prowess/emotional intimacy

❏ How and how much time you spend with your children or with others

This deflecting behavior serves to take the spotlight off whatever they're doing. The sex addict contrives to protect their addiction and may shift the focus to your actions so that you won't notice their sexual acting out. This strategy often works! An addict once told me: "I lie. I cheat. I steal. And these are just some of my good qualities!"

Exercise 3: What I Now See

The blinders are off. What is now entirely apparent to you? Don't censor yourself.

The Impact of Sex Addiction

Like any dependency, our partner's compulsive sexual behavior profoundly impacts us in every aspect of our lives. Here's how another person's sex addiction can directly affect us as intimate partners:

- We feel shame.
- We experience low self-esteem.
- We feel unattractive.

- We doubt our emotions, our sanity, and what we're seeing or what we think we're seeing.
- We feel betrayed by the person we love most. We feel humiliated and stupid for not cluing in sooner.
- We experience abuse and neglect: emotional, sexual, financial, and physical.
- We're worried about the possibility of exposure to sexually transmitted diseases, some of them life-threatening.
- We're afraid to reach out to others for help, fearing what they'll think of us or what they'll think of the sex addict.
- We react by denying or minimizing the sex addiction and its impacts.
- We stuff our feelings around our partner's sex addiction, becoming emotionally numb.
- We feel abandoned.
- We try to talk ourselves out of it by thinking: "He's not like that." or "She'd never do that."
- We try to change, fix, or control the sex addict's behavior by lying and covering up for them, spying on them, checking up on them, eavesdropping on their private conversations, monitoring their computer activity, or by begging, pleading, and even threatening them.
- To please the addict, we may have even participated in sex or sexual activities that feel uncomfortable or unenjoyable. We ultimately feel ashamed of ourselves.
- We blame ourselves for this kind of treatment and for the addict's behavior: "If only I were sexy enough."

- We try controlling the addict and their behavior, and we neglect ourselves and our own lives.
- We misuse drugs, alcohol, food, money, etc., to salve our pain. We may even find ourselves experiencing co-addiction.
- We neglect our own needs, lives, and interests by failing to maintain a connection with our hobbies, our jobs, our children, our health, our families, and our friends.

When faced with someone else's compulsive sexual behavior, you doubt yourself and your sanity rather than questioning the chaotic dysfunction and how it's affecting you. Addiction is crazy and crazy-making!

> An addict once told me: "I lie. I cheat. I steal. And these are just some of my good qualities!"

Kevin's sex addiction mired Molly in a dysfunction fraught with many of the characteristics listed above. Molly shared one particularly glaring feature: "I developed a dependency of my own: an addiction to an online multi-player role-playing game that imitates real life. I'd spend hours online creating a world based on an avatar or character. It became my escape. It's now clear that my online activities mirrored those of my addicted partner." Molly recalls the dopamine rush: "Playing the game felt heady. I dropped my ordinarily enjoyable activities."

An extrovert by nature, Molly no longer wanted to socialize with friends: "I isolated myself. Hours would pass in my alternate world. I couldn't pull myself away from the mesmerizing game. I stopped eating and sleeping properly." After three years and several unsuccessful attempts to cease her escape pattern, Molly finally ended the chaos cold turkey.

Sometimes, to cope with a partner's addiction, we may engage in unhealthy behaviors to salve our pain. When Molly realized that she, too, was falling into the destructive dissociative impact of this online game, she made a conscious decision to stop: "I began to deal with the life I'd been avoiding—the one in real-time, the one that wasn't working for me. I recall telling my anonymous 'friends' that I was ready to leave this online life to resolve my actual reality."

Joan's Story

When Joan's husband was in his full-fledged sex addiction, she found herself seeking out the company of other men: "I sought love and attention, finding this in a series of online relationships that never materialized into real-life experiences. Through lots of flirting and sex chats with men in chat rooms, I was trying to fulfill a need that my relationship couldn't meet."

***

Joan had been experiencing co-addiction involving an addiction to love. Love addiction is the filling of a void with sex in the hopes of feeling loved. Love addiction is common in women and partners of sex addicts. Sex addicts can also be love addicts.

It's bewildering the way one becomes caught in the grip of and mimics someone's addiction without realizing it. In soothing her distress, Molly experienced the erosion of her life: "I was on autopilot in my upset relationship. I felt irritable and confused and devoid of joy. In turn, I'd developed my own compulsive coping behavior." Over time, Molly became more and more conscious of the fact that her relationship with Kevin was not helping her to be her best self: "In fact, it had the potential to destroy me, just as, in the past, my mother's life was swallowed up!"

When Molly finally acknowledged that this chaos was wreaking havoc in her life, she made a firm decision: "I'll change. This very intention would eventually put in motion a series of events that would lead to my massive life transition."

A Legacy of Addiction

The literature about recovery from sex addiction suggests that the family pattern and dynamics we grew up with may have set the scene for future addictive and dysfunctional behaviors. Partners of sex addicts may feel they identify with any of the following family patterns or dynamics:

- We grew up in families where there were secrets—no-talk rules were in place (the elephant in the room phenomenon).
- We learned that our own needs were unimportant and that we should dismiss them.
- We dealt with lots of anger, fear, and depression in ourselves and our close family members. We felt bruised inside.
- We felt isolated from others and alone with our problems.
- We made friendship/relationship choices that were unhealthy and unsupportive.
- We acquired unhealthy beliefs about ourselves during childhood. For example, "My job is to make others happy."
- We received the message that we were unlovable or unworthy.
- We sought/bought love by rescuing others and people-pleasing.

When we learn about our partner's sex addiction, it can be helpful to consider where other examples of addictive behavior exist in our lives. Is there a legacy of addiction in your family of origin? Sometimes family members, including those from past generations, engage in compulsive and dysfunctional behaviors.

Molly highlighted the stories in her family of origin that pointed to a legacy of hurtful, exploitative sexual behavior, abuse, and dysfunction. This legacy established a terrible template and relentlessly groomed Molly to tolerate unhealthy patterns of relating: "I recall my mom telling me about my alcoholic grandfather watching her wash the walls in her new apartment and chanting: 'Oh, baby, up a bit!' as her blouse rose when she reached up. Another story Mom told me was about my great-grandfather teaching my toddler cousin to lower and raise the zipper fly on his pants while sitting on his lap."

Molly came from a family where alcoholism spanned three generations of males. She'd heard about family violence involving her paternal grandfather toward his wife, Molly's grandmother, and his son, Molly's father. Unhealed from his unaddressed abuse, her father perpetuated this terrible legacy. "He physically and verbally abused my dear mother, my innocent younger brother, and me," finished Molly. But she hadn't finished: "Mom told me that my alcoholic father was possessive and jealous. He tracked her down as she was ending an evening out with the girls, chasing her home by car. Once home, he forced sex on her. He raped her!"

Molly shared another revelation that perhaps had shaped her life: "After Mom died, my father remarried within the year. I later learned that my stepmother complained about my father insisting on sex with her every single day. It seems I came from a sex-addiction background and had no clue!"

How would Molly know? How would any of us know this about our parents?

As Molly delved further into the impact of family stories, she began to parallel Kevin's background with her own: "I learned about Kevin's absentee workaholic father who secretly viewed porn and drank alcohol. He had a nervous breakdown and wasn't present to Kevin during his critical teen years. I also learned that after her numerous miscarriages, Kevin's mother placed Kevin on a pedestal when he finally arrived. She was always telling me how her son was perfect!"

What image was Kevin trying to uphold? Molly said that Kevin experimented with sex and marijuana in his early teens, dabbling in harder drugs by the time he was a young adult: "Eventually, alcohol became his go-to substance. Years later, Kevin tried marijuana again at a party. Not long after, he began using it daily."

There were likely other unaddressed, ignored compulsive behaviors and dysfunctions contributing to the legacy of **Whatever we don't deal with stockpiles for the next generation to face.** addiction in both Molly's and Kevin's families of origin. Molly had wondered how all this unhealed energy influenced and shaped Kevin's dependencies: "It seems like no coincidence that we would meet to face our collective demons together! Sounds screwed up, doesn't it?" said Molly.

When we decide to become a couple, we are joining two people's families of origin's baggage, which includes dysfunctional behaviors. After all, whatever we don't deal with stockpiles for the next generation to face. "It was up to me to heal and change the blueprint of my legacy, which was weighted down by Kevin's."

Molly was now conscious that the scales registered this double burden. Addiction had reached a tipping point.

Molly made her decision: "When I was growing up, the focus was on my mother's physical illness and my father's mental illness and addiction. Then as an adult, my focus was on Kevin and his addictions and rituals. I was tired of living with dysfunction and focusing on unwellness." Molly chose to say `Yes' to herself, to healing, and to changing her legacy for generations to come. She didn't want her child to inherit all manner of unresolved trauma. "Unburdened and free, my lightness, my happiness, and my hope will serve as a positive, healthy template." That was Molly's dearest wish for her daughter as she healed herself from a legacy of decades of abuse, alcoholism, and sex addiction.

Exercise 4: Family Legacy of Addiction

Are there any incidents from your family of origin where you've noticed compulsive or dysfunctional behaviors? What were they?

While this is not a witch hunt to assign blame, it is an awareness exercise.

When You Discover the Intimate Betrayal

Once you discover the details of the secret life your partner has been hiding, you may find that you're on high alert. In the past, you may have missed or denied clues. Now you're aware and consciously looking for them. At this point, you:

- Become hypervigilant, like a detective looking for signs and clues that your partner is engaging in the sexual acting out behaviors. You may find yourself checking computer web browsers, telephone bills, cellphone applications, call logs/bills, and credit card statements and asking others about your partner's whereabouts.

- Spend much of your time trying to piece together unrelated behavior to analyze present and predict future episodes of sexual acting out.

- Become distressed when your partner looks at someone else, surfs the Internet, takes a phone call in private, or otherwise engages in behavior associated with the sexual acting out.

- Experience sudden rapid mood shifts, from depression to crying to anger to sadness.

- May be easily triggered by events that relate to your partner's sexual acting out.

- Attempt to rearrange your environment (including your approach to sexual relations with your partner) so that your partner may not be 'tempted' to act out.

- Feel obsessed with the trauma and find it hard to focus and concentrate on other areas of your life. You may find that you're easily distracted.

- Entertain obtrusive fantasy thoughts about your partner's sexual acting out and the betrayal.

- Experience sleeplessness and fatigue — over-thinking might keep you awake at night and occupy your daily thoughts (See obsessive feelings above).

- Isolate from others and avoid even talking about the trauma.

- Question yourself, playing over and over in your mind, different scenarios while trying to manage your self-doubt.

Molly admitted that after discovering Kevin's intimate betrayal, and despite knowing she was leaving him, she was still on high alert. Molly looked for evidence and other instances of Kevin's sexual acting out: "I became hypervigilant. When the door creaked open late at night, my ears perked up. Was he going outside to smoke pot or to peep in windows? At last, I felt validated. I wanted out of this toxic relationship. I wanted out of Kevin's home with a burning desire I'd never experienced before!"

Codependency and Addiction

Codependency occurs when we excessively rely on a partner, either emotionally or psychologically. Typically, this partner is not well and requires support because of an illness or an addiction. Also called co-addiction, codependency refers to the complex interrelationship between addicts and their partners. It is the opposite of healthy interdependence. The partner is entangled in the addict's life in such a way as to be profoundly affected by their actions. They have difficulty functioning, primarily when the addict is acting out or is in crisis.

In her memoir, *A History of a Pedophile's Wife*, Canadian author Eleanor Cowan reflects upon her marriage to a sex addict: "I made his life far more important than the one I hid from—my own" (2013). A partner who makes the addict's life a priority above their own unleashes a pathological loyalty that further destroys the lives of both partners.

"One evening, a member of my support group said that if an addict is a slave, then the addict's partner is a slave of the slave," recalled Molly.

Co-addicts are driven to fix or rescue the addict. A co-addict depends upon the addict for validation. The co-addict may be addicted to the addict. They work hard to control the addict's actions while putting up a positive front for others to see. For example, one member of Molly's support group said she'd regularly host special Sunday dinners for her abusive addict's family in her attempt to present an 'all is well' atmosphere. But all was not well—and this was her cover-up.

The co-addict's dependency issues may stem from unhealed patterns established with addicts in their family of origin. They learned at a very young age that they had to earn another person's love. They learned to be seen and not heard. They came to believe that if they'd only behave in a specific (right) way, then the addict would change.

"When I was a young child, I'd audit my parent's drinking/Rummoli game nights with friends, and my father would tell me that little children are to be seen and not heard!" Molly said. "Later on, I learned to rescue Mom because she was ill and battered by my father," Molly related.

If you find yourself aware of the sex addict's acting out, yet tolerate it as you feel compelled to fix and focus on the addict, you may be experiencing co-addiction. Here are some of the behaviors of the codependent partner:

- Rescuing the addict
- Making excuses for them
- Pleading/bargaining with others on behalf of the addict
- Covering up or lying for them
- Watching or watching out for them (hypervigilance)
- Obsessing about the sex addict and their behavior
- Putting your own life on hold or in jeopardy to do any of the above

- Engaging in compulsive behavior(s) related to any of the above

Pay attention to your actions. Are you engaging in any of these behaviors to avoid looking at yourself and working on your own life? Refrain from blaming and shaming yourself. You can only do the best you can with what you have (See Breaking a habit in Holistic Healing Activities and Practices in Chapter 5).

Jessica's Story

Jessica realized that by posting bail for her partner, Andrew, she'd freed him to return to the streets to flash naked from the waist down in front of young girls. The third time this happened, painful as it was for her, Jessica let Andrew experience the full consequences of his actions. Andrew was not a happy camper (camping out in jail). He threatened divorce. Imagine what a favor he was about to do for Jessica! For her part, Jessica expressed her relief that at least she now knew where her husband was!

***

Not all partners of sex addicts are co-addicted. Many people feel completely blindsided when they first discover the actions of their sex-addicted partners—they did not see this coming from a mile away! And there's a good reason for this: the sexual acting out, like any addiction, may start slowly. It also mirrors abuse in this way. As the addict feels the urge more and more to satisfy an essentially unfillable void, the sexual acting out intensifies—their attempts at covering up also become more elaborate, like telling a lie to cover a lie. As the addiction escalates, so does the sex addict's risk-taking behavior. It's bound to get noticed over time as the sex addict becomes sloppier about covering their tracks, a hallmark of the disease spinning out of control.

Molly recounted that Kevin's pornography consumption transitioned into invasively ogling women in public and then turned into active voyeurism. His addiction incrementally escalated to riskier behavior. "He got sloppy," said Molly. "He left his binoculars in such a suspect place!" Kevin's sexual acting out had intensified, moving into illegal behavior. Molly learned from a police officer that 20 percent of such predators go on to commit more heinous unlawful acts. The question hanging in the air: "Is Kevin part of that 20 percent?" The police, unwilling to take any chances, were on it. Kevin knew they'd be watching.

There is a point, known as hitting bottom, that represents the lowest an addict sinks before getting help (and still, an addict may have to hit bottom many times). According to Molly, getting caught jump-started a change in Kevin. He entered recovery. "Although too late for our relationship," Molly explained, "I've heard it said that when one person goes into recovery, the whole family benefits." By coming out of denial, Molly set off a chain reaction that caused a domino effect of healing.

Margie's Story

Margie was married to Richard for two years. They shared a home with Margie's three teenage children from her previous marriage. After a police raid involving the removal of all computers and cell phones, she learned that Richard faced charges of distributing child pornography. Had Margie seen this coming? Were there any signs? If there were, Richard had hidden them well. But at some point, Richard's deviant behavior had escalated. The law closed in on him and his illegal participation in this multi-billion-dollar-a-year global industry.

***

So how could you, as a partner, have possibly enabled a behavior that you didn't see or about which you didn't know? The trickery of addiction—the dual or double life—is also called the illusory truth effect, the tendency to believe information as being correct after repeated exposure to that information. The sex addict reinforces the illusion of himself or herself as an upstanding citizen in such a way that their double life does not jibe—even when it does come to light (See more about denial in Chapter 4).

Often people cling to old truths because their minds are so conditioned to believe what they know 'to be true.' We've seen this recently with celebrities and in the momentum of the #MeToo Movement. Yes, on some level, mass enabling has occurred, but the illusory effect was equally strong and counterbalancing. We've witnessed 'America's Favorite Dad' played over and over on the television screen, and this image does not fit with the criminal predator, a somnophiliac accused of drugging and raping scores of women. We now see how easily sexual predators hide behind their false personas as pillars of the community.

Use this next reflection activity as an opportunity to review and identify some of your ways of responding to your partner's sexual acting out and how to instead respond to yourself.

Exercise 5: Rescuing and Enabling

1. How do I rescue or enable my sex addict partner?

2. What specific steps am I prepared to take to stop rescuing and enabling the sex addict?

3. How can I instead rescue and prioritize myself?

Sexual Anorexia

A widely held view exists that the sex addict always wants sex and with their partner—a myth that is far from the truth. In many relationships where one partner is sexually acting out outside the couple, they are also withholding sex from their partner. A primary reason is that the addict satisfies their sexual appetite elsewhere. Know that you cannot possibly compete with the addict's sexual fantasies. The sex addict may alternately starve the couple relationship of sexual intimacy and then dive into binge sex. It can be confusing to have lots of sex with your partner and then no sex for protracted periods.

Molly explained how the sexual starving in her relationship with Kevin went on for years: "I couldn't understand the lack of sexual intimacy, the roller-coaster type of sex life that caused so much self-doubt and made me question my desirability and 'enoughness.' Kevin's withholding of sexual intimacy felt punishing and crazy-making. I felt continually rejected, which caused me a lot of emotional pain." Given the old ingrained notions that women aren't supposed to take the lead sexually or even want sex, Molly curtailed her confrontations about the lack of sexual expression.

Years passed, and Molly noticed a shift in her sex life with Kevin: "Suddenly, sexual intimacy became more frequent, which was the opposite of famine, and more like a bulimic gorging on sex. At times, it was too much. I know: *What? Too much? Are you crazy?* Some might say."

Was Molly merely relieving a sexual buildup in the sex addict? Was she Kevin's release from the cumulative failure of his empty voyeuristic activities? "In retrospect, when I learned about Kevin's sexual acting out, I'd felt that he'd treated me like the last repository. Kevin was livid when I told him this, but I was undeterred; I was finally naming what I felt!"

Exercise 6: The Impacts of Someone Else's Sexual Behavior

How has your partner's sexual acting out affected you and your life?

Let's recap the signs that you are dealing with a sex-addicted partner:

- Your life and your relationship feel chaotic.
- You sense that something is not quite right, and you can't figure it out.
- There appears to be a lot of secrecy surrounding your partner's activities.
- The rhythm of your household and your daily routine are dictated by the sex addict and his or her behavior/rituals.
- You feel embarrassed, ashamed, and humiliated by your partner's sexual behavior.
- You tune in to the isolation. You, your family, and your partner seem to be drifting away from your family, friends, and community.
- Time and money remain unaccounted for, if not in short supply, and you can't understand why.

- There are feelings of tension, irritability, and resentment between you and your partner, children, and extended family members, the exact source of which is unknown.
- Promises and agreements made by your partner are often broken or disregarded.
- You feel manipulated, exploited, abused, neglected, and disrespected by your partner.
- You feel dissatisfied with your sex life with your partner.
- People around you have noticed that something is wrong and have told you what they've seen. You may have brushed off their concerns or offered excuses.
- You've followed your partner to/and from places, rescued them from jail, covered for them with their employer, or generally had to cover for their behavior and make more excuses for it.
- You encounter outright lies and lies of omission from your partner.
- You feel emotionally abandoned in the relationship. You are the one doing all the work to keep it going.
- You blame and question yourself. You try too hard.
- You feel isolated and unable to reach out to others out of fear or shame.
- You feel unhappy with your life.
- You do not feel safe and secure in your home and relationship.
- You mistrust your partner. You may even find yourself inquiring about them with others and searching through their personal effects, computer, car, etc., for clues.
- You feel low self-esteem.

- Things seem to be getting worse.
- You feel exhausted as the wheels in your head are continuously spinning, and you often feel anxious.
- You regularly entertain thoughts about leaving your partner.

Molly said that many of these signs resonated with her: "The one that still stands out is the way Kevin and his addictions dictated the rhythm of our household. One issue was dinner hour, a painfully protracted period in our home. Dinner was ready to eat at what was a reasonable hour of six in the evening, especially given the fact that we had a growing child who'd been active all afternoon. But this family time became chronically distressful. This hour was so chaotic that it defies all logic. I'd cook supper, and Kevin would emerge from his home office where he'd been surfing porn. He'd open a beer, then decide to add a dish to the evening fare. My cooking, of course, was not good enough. Sometimes he'd hover and ask if I was following a recipe. The new dish would require extra time to prepare. Even though the complete meal I'd made was ready to eat, we now had to wait for Kevin first to have a beer, then open a bottle of wine, and finally, to cook his contribution to the meal. We'd feel hungry and frustrated. The idea was to preserve the family mealtime. Under the guise of honoring dinners together, wait we did."

"Finally seated, Kevin drank more wine and monopolized the dinner conversation, spouting off about spiritual principles. Sometimes there'd be 'IQ tests' as Kevin questioned his family about something only he knew the answer to, like a trick question. It felt as if Kevin was dumbing me down. He'd also do this to friends and family at social gatherings."

Not uncommonly, in cases of addiction, acting superior to others is a way of covering up one's feelings of insecurity or issues of not feeling good enough. When we act morally superior to others, we may be trying to mask our deep-seated feelings of inadequacy.

Author of *The Psychology of Secrets*, Anita E. Kelley, advises: "So the next time someone acts arrogant and makes you feel dumb or unattractive, ask yourself, 'What shortcoming is this person masking?' At least this way you can short-circuit their making you feel bad about yourself" (2010).

By the time dinner was eaten and the kitchen cleaned, it was 9:30 pm — and sometimes even later. "Most evenings followed this skewed schedule. It was worse in the summertime because Kevin's outdoor barbecuing would take longer."

Molly assumed total responsibility for picking up their daughter from a school friend's home since Kevin couldn't drive when he'd been drinking: "We'd rarely go out in the evening because this disrupted Kevin's drinking rituals. I was dealing with someone who always had to have his way. And he'd always find a way to get his way!"

In general, there was an unhealthy atmosphere of tension and resentment in Molly and Kevin's relationship and their household. "I resented Kevin for what he could not give to me and vice versa. I was the giver, the peacemaker, and the one who would smooth things over for the benefit of our family." Reminiscent of her childhood pattern of rescuing and taking care of her family, Molly would 'pretzel' herself by trying to live up to all the expectations — justifying and people-pleasing at the same time. "Again, I was working hard at being good enough in the face of such insanity!"

Through her tolerance of Kevin's control, her rescuing efforts, and her protracted endurance of Kevin's disrespect, Molly enabled

Kevin to have things his way so that his addictions could lead. Molly recounted her anger at what she'd tolerated: "I allowed Kevin to dictate the rhythm of our household. Once I clued in to how crazy this chaos was—although not yet to the sex addiction driving it—I was outraged and fed up! Finally, I understood the source of all my resentment and pent-up anger, and I realized that I'd need to be the one to change if things were to change. So, I established a new routine. I'd prepare dinner for my child and me. We ate at six in the evening, regardless of what Kevin did. I left him to his own devices."

Another change Molly made was going out in the evenings to attend writing classes and support group meetings. This restored essential equilibrium and sanity for Molly: "I took back my life and my power. It was no longer about Kevin, but about my priorities."

Reaching Out for Support

You're in deep water, and you're drowning. Someone sees you and throws you a buoy. Your survival instinct is so strong that you don't question whether you should grab onto this lifeline. You do, and you feel relieved as you're pulled back to safety. Know that there are many options for recovery from the devastating impact of intimate betrayal: rehabilitation programs, therapy, recovery programs, and support groups for both the sex addict and for the partner who has been affected by the intimate betrayal.

Keeping secrets keeps us sick in our dysfunction. If you feel isolated and alone with the problem of dealing with the sex addict, it can be helpful to reach out to others who are experiencing a similar situation. When you share your story with another person, you may discover common aspects of your experiences. You begin to realize that you're not alone with your pain.

A support group can help you cope with your intimate partner's sex addiction. Support groups are safe, confidential spaces where you can go to share your struggles and gains and grow in your learning about sex addiction. Although not all people's experiences and circumstances are the same, you share the common bond of a relationship with a sex addict that adversely affects your life. You may learn that:

- You are not alone. Other people live through intimate betrayal.
- You aren't crazy. You're dealing with a crazy situation.
- You deserve more and better.
- You are worthy and lovable.
- You are strong and capable.
- The sex addict's actions do not define you as a person.

Although you may be questioning yourself in the face of this chaos, you are a competent and caring human being who excels in so many areas of your life, and you come to realize that:

- You may have been relying on someone who can't meet your need for love, intimacy, and sharing.
- You cannot control people, places, and things related to the sex addict's compulsive acting out.
- You can learn to trust yourself and your intuition/ inner voice.
- You must prioritize yourself and your needs by focusing on yourself and your own life.
- You have choices.

Let's repeat the message here: This is not your fault. You did not cause your partner to act out sexually. You cannot control whether they continue to act out sexually or choose to stop and get help.

Connecting with other people can break the pattern of isolation as we spiral downward into the pit of our partner's sex addiction. By talking with others, we share our pain, which eventually lessens because it's no longer ours alone to bear.

Reaching out to a support group can help you deal with your partner's sexual acting out. If there is no group available in your area, find an online group. There are Internet forums and chat rooms where you can find support without leaving home.

Molly had been attending a recovery group to deal with Kevin's drinking. When she first discovered his sexual acting out, Molly contacted another group, one for partners of sex addicts. The invaluable support this group offered helped Molly in many ways: "I heard stories, and although the details may have been different from mine, all of them held the common elements of intimate betrayal and the pain of being repeatedly deceived. I was no longer alone with my suffering! Support also helped me tell my story. In telling it, my authority increased."

Exercise 7: Join a Support Group

Find a support group for partners of sex addicts. There exist both in-person and online meeting options. If you feel more comfortable or cannot find a group that meets face-to-face, investigate an online group (See Websites under Recommended Resources at the end of this book).

If you do already attend a support group, how does this help you?

You've been affected by someone else's compulsive sexual behavior over which you have no control. But you do have control over YOU and your priorities. How empowering is *that*?

Chapter 3

Living the Cycle of Abuse

It may not feel as though this chapter about abuse applies to you and your situation. After all, you're experiencing the effects of someone's addiction. Know that abuse can intertwine with sexual acting out. Betrayal is ultimately abuse. Although not all sex addicts are outright abusive, the nature of addiction is abusive. In this chapter, we'll look at the nuances.

Abuse, also referred to as domestic violence or intimate partner violence (IPV), can be physical, emotional, sexual, verbal, and financial. Abuse can include neglect or any act of violence against you and your children by your intimate partner. The cycle of abuse can mirror the cycle of addiction. Making this link is essential to understanding the complexity of sex addiction.

The Cycle of Abuse

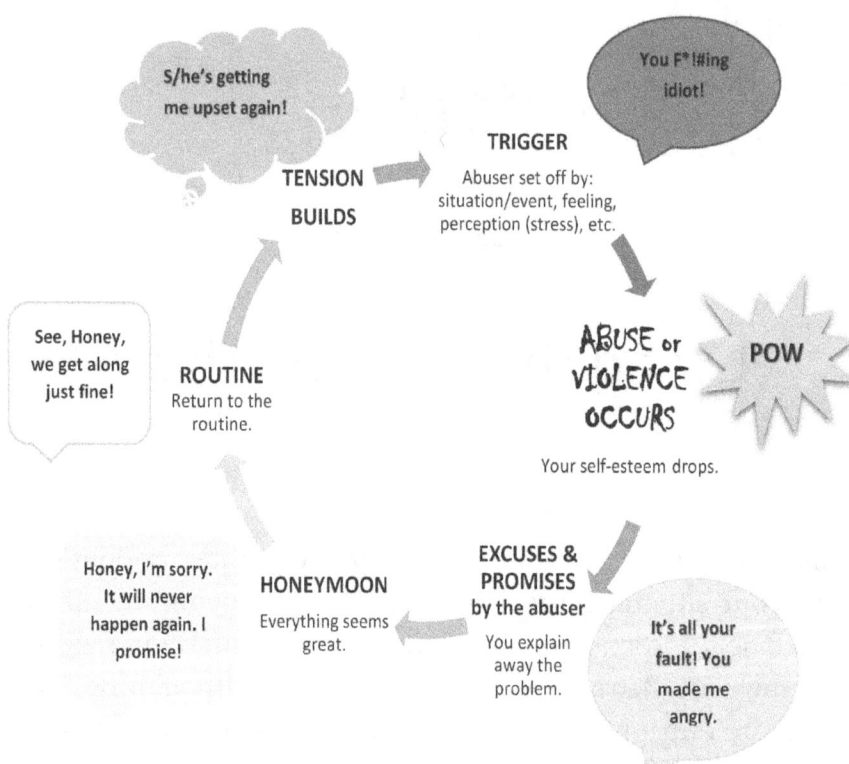

Figure 2: Adaptation of Dr. Lenore E. Walker's Cycle of Abuse

The graphic above depicts the cyclical pattern of abuse, according to Dr. Lenore E. Walker's social theory developed in 1979. A pioneering force, Dr. Walker coined the term "Battered Woman Syndrome." Adapted from Walker's four phases, this cycle also parallels the circular pattern of compulsive acting out that sex addicts follow. The abuse cycle follows a predictable pattern where excuses and promises supersede abusive or violent acts. Afterward, there's a return to the routine, and everything seems peaceful. Eventually, tension builds and is released when a triggering event or situation occurs just before the abuse erupts once again.

As the cycle of abuse continues, your self-esteem drops. This sets the stage for you to feel like you're not good enough or enough. It slowly happens over time as you experience and tolerate the abuse. You may not even be aware of it because you're fighting an uphill battle coping with the incidences of abuse.

While not all addicts are directly physically or emotionally abusive, the nature of addiction involves both neglect and abuse. The chaos inherent in addictive behavior doesn't vary. Addicts lie, cheat, and manipulate to protect their habits. They may not intentionally set out to abuse you, but their acting out contains elements of abuse. Caught in the cycle of addiction, they may be either unaware or actively aware. The addict may be able to acknowledge what's happening, but at the same time, feels powerless to change it.

Back to Molly's Journey

Molly's legacy predetermined her physical abuse template. Molly explained that it began while she was in her mother's womb: "According to Mom, I wasn't supposed to be born. When he found out she was pregnant with me, my father made Mom take hot baths to induce a miscarriage. He wasn't ready for a child. They were building their home, the one that was never fully finished, even by the time I moved out in my early twenties. Mom obeyed, running the water as hot as she could bear," recounted Molly.

Despite this cruelty, Molly said she survived: she was born a month early and weighed only four pounds and a few ounces. And that transgression, Molly's father's initial misogynistic treatment of his wife—and his daughter in utero—was just the first of many he'd perpetrate against Molly and her mother. The groundwork was laid: "It established a pattern that was to follow me throughout my life."

"Mom told me I was a happy baby, cooing to myself in my crib well before the morning alarm would signal the start of my father's workday. She said that I even laughed," Molly said.

> **While not all addicts are directly physically or emotionally abusive, the nature of addiction involves both neglect and abuse.**

If ignorance is bliss, then a cooing baby is blissfully ignorant of the harsh realities of the world, as Molly would come to understand, first through being abused at home, then at school, and later in her couple relationship.

"I grew up in a home that was a construction zone by day and a war zone at night. I'd awaken to the sound of power tools and loud music on weekends as my father renovated the house, a bottle of beer always close at hand. I'd fall asleep to violent arguments between my parents. These arguments resulted in Mom climbing into my bed, where the angry tirade would continue. I would run interference between my parents while deprived of sleep."

"I grew older and stronger. I'd help my father by holding up a T-bar made of two-by-fours to support sheets of Gyprock as he screwed them to the ceiling. I can't remember if my father was finally finishing part of the house or ripping it out because it wasn't perfect. All the family photographs from my childhood depict bare walls with plaster spots covering nails and joints, except the one where my childhood artwork covered a punch hole made by my father's heavy fist. I'd have colored entire murals if it meant he'd beat the walls instead of my mother and me," Molly explained.

"Mom knit me slippers from 'Phentex,' a twisted chemical yarn-blend, which she insisted we wear to walk on Dad's perpetually unfinished floors. The exposed plywood became brittle and weak due to repeated washings with bleach and hot water. Tiny wooden splinters would lodge into my thinly protected feet through the fragile loose-knit fabric. I spent many painful moments as my mother extracted the jagged shards from my wounded feet."

Today, Molly sees the symbolism: "As powerless as she was, my mother sought to minimize the damage to my feet. That was the limit of what she could do. It was beyond Mom's emotional capability to command her aggressive partner to finish the damn floors." Molly's mother couldn't shout "Enough!" because, in her ravaged self, she was not 'enough.'

Molly explained her father's physical abuse: "My father would beat me for stupid reasons. As a child, I once shared cookies from our pantry with the children across the street. They came from a family of nine, where snacks were scarce. Food was plentiful in our home. I took the cookies outside to eat with my friends in their playhouse. I thought it a fair exchange for a few delightful hours in their cool structure. Later that evening, when my father found out, he beat me black and blue. I remember the next day, going to the corner store for beer for our family abuser, and telling the 'Store Lady,' as we used to call her, that I'd been hit playing baseball. Blue rings circled my eyes. The bigger bruise—the one she couldn't see—throbbed on my right buttock. My clothing hid more welts from that merciless lashing. She asked me if I was sure. Telling the truth felt scary, so I lied." Molly acknowledged her cover-up.

Caught between the need to be safe and the wish to be loyal to her family, Molly was both battered by and tied to protecting her abuser. Misplaced, pathological loyalty had taken root.

Food presented contradictions for Molly: "Now reluctant to share my food with others, I'd eat to salve my pain and to comfort myself. This pattern continued, and my weight fluctuated throughout adulthood. Later I learned the joy of making and sharing meals with people I love." Molly related this twisted irony.

She further explained how her home life continued to be very rough: "Mom was chronically ill. My father acted out violently toward Mom and me. I became the family caretaker from a young age, tending to my sick mother, rescuing her from my father's violent outbursts, looking after my younger brother, and doing household chores."

At school, Molly suffered bullying: "It started in the gym locker room late in elementary school when, learning of my self-consciousness about my budding breasts, a group of girls began to call me 'Chester.' Two older kids regularly threatened to beat me up as I got off the school bus. One time, a small group of classmates banded together during a library research visit and taunted me because my last name was the same as a famous hanged criminal." Molly recalled the violence that formed the tapestry of both her home and school life.

In retrospect, this ill-treatment by her peers was no surprise to Molly. Statistically, children abused at home often become targets for bullies at school. Sandwiched between two violent worlds, Molly had no safe harbor.

"I'd also experienced sexual abuse: on three occasions, I met exhibitionists who'd stop their cars to expose their penises. In grade school, a male classmate poked me in my crotch when we were alone in the classroom. My home life and school experiences groomed me for a dysfunctional couple relationship." Molly explained her continuous oppression.

Most parents want their children to be happy. Ideally, they wish that their children will find partners who will honor, love, protect, and respect them. Molly's self-absorbed father couldn't model those positive traits for her. His violence toward Molly impacted her self-esteem and taught Molly to tolerate ill-treatment from others.

Through his drinking and abuse, Molly's father primed her to seek out an abusive partner who would also salve his pain with substances: "At first, believing I'd chosen a partner who was completely different from my father, I didn't even notice the mistreatment. Issues I hadn't resolved with my father reappeared in my couple relationship. Physically and emotionally, I was unwell from my abusive childhood. I became a prime candidate to enter into a partnership with someone just as ill as my father."

This pattern was deeply entrenched. Molly chose an addicted and abusive partner who could not commit to her. "Marriage was never an option because every time I expressed my interest in getting married, Kevin sidestepped the issue."

Molly recalled the early verbal abuse, citing a particularly nasty remark Kevin made following the birth of their daughter: "When I lamented how my body had changed and that I'd need new clothes, he told me, 'If you want new clothes, you'll have to go back to work.' That retort stung, and it cut me to my core. I remember the feeling of insecurity that settled in the pit of my stomach." That dagger proved to be one of many hurtful comments that chipped away at Molly's self-esteem and her trust in her couple relationship with Kevin.

"Kevin knew better than to lay a hand on me physically," Molly said. "Physical violence was my deal-breaker boundary, one that if crossed, meant he'd lose control of the myriad other ways he had me shackled in our abusive relationship. In retrospect, we looked to each other to fill our respective voids. Just as my father found me unworthy, my partner mirrored that reality. That was normal to me."

It would take Molly many years to leave this unhealthy dynamic of emotional and verbal abuse. "A parting comment Kevin made to me just before I left summed up his nastiness and lack of commitment: 'If I'd wanted to give you half my wealth, I'd have married you.'" Molly finally realized that Kevin couldn't do for her what she could not do for herself.

The Abusive Nature of Addiction

Let's look at some examples of the abusive nature of addiction as it plays out in the life of Oliver, first presented in Chapter 1.

Oliver's Story

Megan engages in sex chats on the computer. Her husband, Oliver, is aware of Megan's activities when she's acting out sexually. He feels unworthy and as if something is wrong with him. His self-esteem plummets.

Catching her in a sex chat, Oliver confronts Megan; she lies and gives excuses to explain her behavior. Oliver wants the relationship to work so badly that he accepts Megan's explanations. Things go well for a while. Megan is more doting and loving. There's a return to their routine as a couple. But tensions soon build in Megan. She experiences a trigger—maybe stresses at home or work. She ends up in sex chat rooms once again, and the telltale signs are that she begins to distance herself from Oliver and becomes unavailable to him.

This time, though, Megan blames Oliver for her sexual acting out. Her behavior, she insists, is his fault. In effect, Megan gaslights Oliver, causing him to doubt his sanity because of her manipulation. Oliver feels that he's the one with the problem: he tells himself that there wouldn't be a problem if only he was more this way or did that better.

Oliver feels even worse and blames himself. He questions his desirability and his 'enoughness.' He battles childhood demons resulting from his relationship with his standoffish, emotionally unavailable mother who left him with relatives to chase yet another love interest. Oliver's father took off when he was just a toddler. Unhealed from unresolved childhood injuries, Oliver slowly loses his grasp on reality. The cycle starts all over again as Megan continues to connect in the sex chat rooms online. Because Megan does not admit to her behavior or take responsibility for her actions, she continues to act out. Both Megan and Oliver live their respective cycles of addiction and abuse.

***

Let's look at another type of abuse common to partners of sex addicts: financial abuse. Financial abuse occurs when the sex-addicted partner misuses the couple's joint financial resources. Purchasing sexual services or losing income resulting from the sex addict not working, and instead, spending this valuable time to engage in their sexual compulsions can result in unpaid bills and collections agents calling your home. You lose financial stability, and your worries escalate.

Molly's Journey Continues

"What does your partner do?" Molly's colleague asked during a coffee break.

"He's a brilliant financial analyst," Molly replied. Inside, Molly cringed at the lie because there were many financially lean years in Molly and Kevin's relationship during which Kevin was either unemployed or underemployed. She couldn't understand how someone with so much education and experience could languish around the house.

Compounding Molly's frustration was the stress of juggling her work reality: "I was mostly self-employed and working on contract. I felt pressure to take on as many jobs as I could, even though my daughter was a preschooler."

Looking back and unbeknownst to her at the time, Molly realized that Kevin's sex addiction might have contributed to his chronic unemployment.

***

Lorna's Story

Lorna couldn't wrap her mind around the frightening fact that she and her husband, Stan, would lose their home. They owned a successful family business that had been doing well. Then Stan began increasingly claiming that they couldn't make ends meet. He insisted that creditors were closing in on them and that the bank would likely repossess their home for mounting unpaid credit card bills. As it turned out, Stan was paying for multiple weekly visits with escorts and prostitutes. Lorna made this shocking discovery when she opened the statement for a little-used joint emergency credit card. There was no mistaking the name of the company debiting the funds. Lorna soon learned the astounding statistic that one in five American men have solicited a prostitute.

When Lorna confronted Stan, he was relieved that his secret was out. The two eventually decided to work through the betrayal and its damaging effects, which included ultimately losing their executive home and having to downsize to a townhouse. Stan sought help through a support group and worked with a mentor to restore his accountability, both to himself and Lorna. Lorna attends a support group for partners of sex addicts.

***

Now, let's look at how addiction amplifies the abuse/violence cycle:

If your partner regularly puts you down or belittles you, it's emotional abuse. As Kevin's addiction progressed, so did his verbal abuse of Molly. He relentlessly criticized her: "Kevin often put me down for the way I dressed and for my weight. If I went out with a friend, he'd comment that I was off having fun while he was working at home," Molly explained.

Kevin's gaslighting was purposely designed to get Molly feeling so bad about herself that she wouldn't notice his sexual acting out. Gaslighting—a tactic someone uses to gain power—plants seeds of doubt. This psychological manipulation ultimately caused Molly to question her perceptions and her sanity.

The most significant form of violence Molly was to experience with Kevin happened when he locked her out of their shared home. One spring Saturday after Molly had let their teenage daughter practice driving the car, Kevin became livid. He had wanted to take driving privileges away as a punishment, and he decided to teach Molly a lesson for opposing his wishes in disciplining their daughter: "He slid the child lock on the front door, barring my entrance. He then left the house via the side door, for which I didn't have the key."

When Molly called the police, they told her that they couldn't let her into the home she shared with Kevin—hearing about this reality compounded her shock. Even though, as a common-law couple, she and Kevin had lived in this house for over a decade, and all her personal belongings and work tools were there, the police couldn't force Kevin to permit Molly entry because the legal ownership deed was in his name. "I'd need a lawyer's letter to gain entry into my home!"

The police met Molly later when Kevin returned: "He refused to open the door. Instead, to appear as if he was not in total obstruction of the law, Kevin left the patio door at the back of the house unlocked. I only discovered this after the police had tried to negotiate with him for close to twenty minutes through an open front window," Molly recounted.

When Molly was able to get back into the house, she quickly packed for herself and her daughter while police escorts waited. She drove to her brother's home for an indeterminate stay: "That night, I felt profoundly homeless. My security had been ripped out from under me. In a matter of hours, Kevin had shattered my feelings of safety and security in our relationship. Over the weeks that followed, I grieved this loss deeply. Something major had shifted." This traumatic experience foreshadowed the events of the following year. As it turned out, this was Molly's practice run at leaving Kevin.

Three days later, Kevin called Molly to apologize. He blamed a backache resulting from a slipped disk for his shocking behavior of locking Molly out of their shared home. Kevin begged Molly to return. He told her that he'd figured she'd use their joint credit card to stay in a hotel for the weekend.

"I was free to use our joint credit card to pay for a hotel, but I wasn't allowed to enter our shared home!" Molly couldn't believe it. To her horror, she'd learned that Canada's provincial laws accord no rights to common-law partners. Kevin had treated Molly like a wayward child who needed to learn a lesson. "I told Kevin I'd think about it, but that for the time being, I was staying away."

Molly explained how she felt hopeless and broken because deep down, she felt a sense of homelessness. She felt so low that her sister-in-law suggested a local support group for partners of alcoholics. That suggestion was the beginning of Molly's emancipation.

A member of the group who eventually became Molly's mentor suggested that she not make any significant change for one year. "Did it mean that I should go back home to Kevin, who by this time, was pleading and bargaining with me?" Molly said. "Or should I continue to stay with my brother? I felt confused. I felt displaced and out of my comfort zone—as uncomfortable as that was!"

It would be three months before Molly returned—against the sage advice of supportive family and friends. "I guess I wasn't ready to leave Kevin yet," she said.

When she'd returned to Kevin, her sister-in-law told Molly that she was welcome back any time. Molly thanked her and said, "Next time, I'll move into an apartment."

Now that Molly was attending a support group, the dysfunction became more evident to her. She began to see what she'd missed or dismissed. She put conditions on her return home to Kevin, mostly unmet ones. "There'd be no cohabitation agreement, but we did write legal wills," said Molly. "And Kevin and I converted a storage room into a home office where I could now work without distraction. I painted it bright yellow. I installed my computer, a desk, and a new sofa bed." Interestingly, by arranging this mini space that would be hers alone, Molly previewed the new home she'd set up a year later when she left Kevin for good. Yellow represents cowardice and deceit on the one hand but stands for freshness, optimism, and loyalty on the other.

Molly was guarded but hopeful: "I made a promise to myself. I vowed that no one would ever again render me homeless."

Molly noticed the honeymoon phase when she returned. When she and Kevin took a short train trip together, a stranger sitting nearby asked if they were on their honeymoon. The cycle of abuse was following its usual patterned course.

It was a rough year for Molly. Her trust in her relationship with Kevin was never fully restored, and although something didn't feel right, Molly still hadn't clued into Kevin's active sex addiction. Later that year, Molly and Kevin sold their joint rental property, and Molly put her share of the money into savings. She explained how Kevin regularly goaded her: "He'd say 'Now that you have money, you'll leave.' I said, 'No,' but part of me wasn't convinced. In fact, over the winter months, I found myself looking at apartments."

One year later, Molly got an opportunity and her ultimate reason to leave Kevin when she made the unsettling discovery of the binoculars.

"After discovering his sexual acting out, as I was preparing to move, Kevin was increasingly distraught that our relationship had declined to this point. One morning, while getting ready for school, our daughter had asked me to text instead of calling since there'd be a better chance of connecting that way.

Right in front of me, Kevin said, 'Don't bother explaining. Your mother can't learn new things.' "Although this venomous barb was one of many I'd become accustomed to hearing, I told Kevin, 'If you don't stop these verbal put-downs, I'll get a lawyer and make it stop!'" Molly said.

"Kevin drove our daughter to school and apologized when he returned, telling me that he had no clue why he lashed out like that," Molly said. "I reminded Kevin that putting me down has always been his default behavior."

It turned out that during the drive, their daughter had told Kevin that he was not helping his case around Molly leaving.

"I knew that despite the excuses, there'd be another incident of verbal abuse, especially with tensions mounting over discovering Kevin's sex addiction." For her part, Molly counted the days until her departure.

Reach Out for Help

Abuse is insidious. Like a snake hiding in the grass, it slithers up on you gradually. Abusers don't declare themselves overtly, but through their hurtful, destructive behavior toward you. After all, you need to be distracted from their smooth moves. Abuse is a dark pit containing many layers of grit. Abusive behavior can take a myriad of forms, including:

- Controlling and manipulating you
- Isolating you from friends and family
- Belittling comments towards you
- Sabotaging you and your efforts
- Guilting you
- Sudden explosive outbursts towards you
- Deflecting personal responsibility

As a partner, you may find yourself having to deal with an abuser's jealousy, intensity, passive-aggressive behaviors, and betrayal. There can be sudden angry outbursts or emotional explosions that hijack you or hit you from nowhere. Emotional hijacking—the sudden unleashing of rage—is hugely damaging to a relationship. You may find yourself fearfully walking on eggshells, not knowing if, when, or how the anger will surface again. You feel powerless because you can't control the other person's angry outbursts.

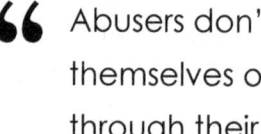
> Abusers don't declare themselves overtly, but through their hurtful, destructive behavior toward you.

All this leaves you questioning yourself. The tricky thing with abuse is that it develops slowly. It catches you off guard; initially, the incidents may be far enough apart that you don't notice the mistreatment right away. You may even make excuses for your abuser, such as:

- He's tired./He just lost control.
- I deserved it./It's my fault.
- She didn't mean it.
- He's not even aware of what he's doing/saying.
- I'm overly sensitive.
- She apologized and said that it wouldn't happen again.

When an incident happens once, you wonder. When it happens a second time, you notice. When it happens again, you see a definite pattern. Often, this is where we second-guess ourselves, thinking that perhaps it's us, that we're the problem.

The put-downs can graduate to outright physical violence. Or not. Subtler and less visible emotional abuse can occur when your partner blames you for their behavior and manipulates you into feeling awful. You then blame yourself for their outburst. You may not even notice how low your self-esteem has become or how unhappy you feel because of it. You're often too distracted with feeling deficient. Guilt, self-blame, self-deprecation, and even depression may be constant companions. And insidiously, feelings of not being good enough creep in.

> When an incident happens once, you wonder. When it happens a second time, you notice. When it happens again, you see a definite pattern.

Self-blame and guilt keep you tethered. The hope that things will change keeps you tied in knots. The fact that you have children keeps you shackled. Financial dependence on your partner keeps you confined. Most likely, it is your fear of the unknown that keeps you trapped.

Molly recalls how fear had kept her bound to a dysfunctional couple relationship: "As Kevin's addiction escalated, I endured more and more verbal onslaughts and emotional abuse. I told myself this was nowhere near as grim as what I'd lived as a child with my alcoholic father. There were no blue bruises on my body."

Moreover, Molly had witnessed her father's insane physical violence toward her mother, who'd felt powerless to leave due to her chronic illness: "Mom was my perfect example of tolerating abuse. Somehow, going it alone seemed foreboding and unthinkable, despite the indisputable fact that I had a thriving career and the ability to provide for myself." Molly had been contributing financially to her family's well-being for years, even covering expenses when Kevin was between jobs. Molly tolerated her unhappiness because it was what she knew: "I had followed the path of least resistance. I'd become familiar with discomfort," she said.

Life has a way of bringing lessons back to us (See Life Tests in Chapter 6). Joseph Campbell explains this reinforcement as a call to action on our hero's journey. Something taps us to get our attention—sometimes that tap turns into a slap to get noticed. "It's interesting how we get the lessons we need in life," stated Molly. "What I didn't get the first time reshaped itself into different forms until I got it."

From her discovery of Kevin's sexual acting out until several months after leaving him, Molly embarked upon an incredible opportunity to work with a nonprofit organization on a project about family violence. The plan involved scoping out a toolkit to enable service providers to help victims of family violence.

A year later, Molly began facilitating discussion panels for these service providers—police, women's shelter workers, and victim-aid organizations—to unveil the toolkit. Through this exposure, Molly faced the stark reality that she, too, was a victim of family violence: "Once more, the universe tapped me on the shoulder—or rather, whacked me on the side of the head—to wake me up to my reality," recalled Molly.

When Molly finally decided to end her collapsed relationship, Kevin's verbal abuse ramped up. "Kevin was frustrated that I'd discovered his sexual acting out and that I'd no longer enable it, much less stay with him."

Molly reached out to a local refuge for abused women. Together they determined that Molly could live under the same roof with

Kevin while making her plans and preparations to leave. It was three months before Molly could move into her new apartment. She explained that she'd confronted Kevin: "I need to know that my belongings and I will be safe for the time I remain here."

Molly participated in excellent weekly individual and group counseling sessions as an out-client of the women's shelter. The immediate goal of counseling was to support her decision to end her relationship with Kevin and help her leave safely. The long-term goal was to help her break the cycle of abuse once and for all.

A searing statistic about domestic violence confirms that partners are most vulnerable to physical abuse or deadly violence just before, during, and immediately after leaving an abusive relationship. Molly decided not to take a chance: "I didn't know whether Kevin would act out violently because of feeling destabilized by my leaving. While preparing to move, I repeatedly told Kevin that I was unwell and needed to leave the relationship to heal." And as a precaution, after Molly left, she didn't divulge her new address.

It can take seven attempts for someone to leave their abusive situation, attempts fraught with fear and doubt: "I know people don't get it, but the abuser manipulates you so that you keep going back. They apologize, and they promise to change. And they do change for a short time, just long enough to keep you off balance and questioning your sanity. You begin to think everything is going well, then they act up again," said Molly.

It's part of the cycle of abuse. Although people cannot understand why someone would tolerate the abuse, much less return once they've left, two factors prevail:

1. The abuser grooms the victim, usually homing in on a vulnerability or weakness.
2. The abuser instills fear in the victim, either overtly or subtly.

Grooming can be anything from compliments to favors, to buying gifts for the victim, making them and their family members feel special in a way they've never experienced. Intimidation may start slowly with implied threats and graduate to overt threats to your safety or the safety of your children/family if you do x, y, or z or if you leave. There can exist a Jekyll and Hyde quality where the abuser presents a kind face to outsiders and another, nasty face to you. And vice versa: the abuser may be sweet with you but mean to someone close to you who challenges them. The difficulty for you is that the abuser may sway family and friends by manipulating them so that they doubt you when you try to tell them that you're being abused.

And then there are the apologies, the excuses, and the promises—coated in self-righteous justifications. Sierra Monaee aptly sums it up: "An apology without change is just manipulation" (*Stop Believing his Apologies*, 2019). The point is that the abuser/manipulator has a chameleon-like ability to control and master any situation to suit their purposes.

Once the victim catches on to the abuse, they are their best assessor of the risks and potential for being harmed. At some point, they may come to realize that their life is in danger. They have a sense of what their partner is capable of—this is where fear can be the driver to either stay or leave. For their part, feelings of desperation or the fear of losing control drive the abuser.

Molly reaffirmed that if she'd learned one thing about her precious mother's tragic abuse, it was that she did not want to be a victim or a casualty of physical violence. Her mother had a severe, painful, and chronic illness, a condition accompanied by the constant threat of death because of surgeries, infections, and complications she suffered. Ultimately, Molly's father's relentless physical, emotional, and verbal attacks quashed her mother's will to live.

"My father snuffed out Mom's spark prematurely. Through telling my story, I'm rekindling my mother's light," Molly stated.

Although this was her legacy, Molly knew that she had the power to change the course of her history. In her early forties, Molly managed to break the cycle that she would not let break her!

Abusive Addicts with Psychological Disorders

The word narcissist is often used to describe the sex addict. Characteristic behaviors of narcissists include:

- Gaslighting
- Isolating you
- Devaluing your efforts
- Denying
- Projecting (It's your fault)
- Controlling
- Invalidating
- Expecting perfection
- Manipulating
- Making threats
- Withholding love and affection
- Refusing to accept accountability
- Having an attitude of entitlement

All these tactics are a betrayal because they are abusive. By design, they invoke an adverse reaction from you. Your response is then used against you and twisted around to make it look like you're the one with the problem.

Characteristics of partners of narcissists include:
- Self-blame
- Self-justification
- Over-apologizing
- Doing whatever you need to keep the peace
- Fueling the narcissist, thus giving them power and control over you

The behaviors outlined above describe much of what Molly experienced from both her father and Kevin. She'd often justify her behavior merely to keep the peace: "It seemed that my whole life was a justification for why I'd survived my abused mother's steaming hot baths," Molly said. "I'd rarely felt any empathy from Kevin. He was emotionally unavailable and withholding. Everything was all about him. Even though I heard much wisdom at my support meetings, at home, I was not invited to share these insights. Instead, Kevin hijacked family dinner conversations with his evangelical proselytizing about the wise words of whatever self-help guru he was currently reading."

By the sounds of it, Kevin appeared to be doing deep inner work necessary to wrestle the demons of his addictions, which was not the case at all. What he was doing was fashioning an elaborate cover. Addicts often hide by manipulating situations so that you see and believe what they want you to see and believe. Molly wondered, "Was this the nature of Kevin's addiction, or was there an underlying undiagnosed psychological disorder at play?"

It's impossible to get a professional diagnosis if your partner refuses to consult. However, do reach out for help for yourself, especially if you feel twisted in your emotional responses.

Molly recalled a wonderfully validating comment from a mediator-counselor who, when they met after Kevin had locked her out, told her that Kevin was someone who always had to have things his way. "Hearing this from a professional who'd seen through many manipulators, was a tremendous relief to me," said Molly. "This counselor had identified the undercurrent that I'd been swimming against for years!"

Molly didn't know whether it was Kevin's addictions, his temperament, or a personality disorder, such as narcissism: "I just knew about the disturbing effects of addiction from years of living with addicts."

While a psychological disorder in the sex addict isn't always apparent, such untreated disturbance can contribute to the complex and abusive nature of addiction. Bipolar disorder, narcissism, psychopathy, and sociopathy are a few personality disorders that may come into play—all of which must be diagnosed by a qualified health care professional.

 Abuse breeds silence through the shame it causes in its victim.

Despite my studies in psychology, I'm reluctant to make pronouncements about an addict's mental health. Although there is some discussion here about the behaviors related to personality disorders, a proper diagnosis of these pathologies extends beyond the scope of this workbook. If you suspect or feel impacted by any of these disorders in your sex-addicted partner, you must seek professional guidance for yourself.

Establish Your Safety Plan

Abuse breeds silence through the shame it causes in its victim. Victims learn to victimize themselves. After a while, the abuser no longer even needs to raise a fist or sling a verbal barb. The insidiousness of abuse keeps its victims chained. If someone treats you disdainfully enough, and you tolerate it, your spirit becomes broken. You keep reliving the cycle and the pain. The only way to end the abuse is to exit the cycle.

If you're dealing with emotional abuse or physical violence from your intimate partner, you must establish a plan for your safety and your safe exit. Developing a safety plan means compiling a list of emergency contact numbers, concealing a bag packed with personal items and necessary documents, and securing a secret place to go if you must leave quickly.

Exercise 8: My Safety Plan

If you had to leave your home suddenly:
- Who would you call?
- What would you bring? (Is this packed and easily accessible?)
- Where would you go?

Develop a safety plan and create a quick exit strategy.

Addictions can intertwine with abuse to form a tangle of dysfunction. All abuse feels dehumanizing.

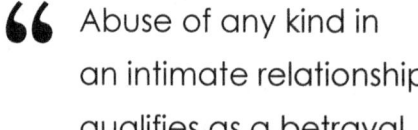 Abuse of any kind in an intimate relationship qualifies as a betrayal.

Abuse diminishes your personhood, your self-esteem, and your trust in yourself. It slowly breaks you down. If the addict is successful in gaslighting you, you'll feel that their addiction and its consequences are your fault, and you'll begin to victimize yourself through self-blame. Some examples include:

- If I hadn't argued with my partner, he wouldn't have left for the night.
- He hit me because I made him angry. I should learn to keep quiet.
- She's back on computer chat again because I had to work overtime tonight.
- I've gained weight. My partner isn't attracted to me. It's my fault he's looking at porn.

You'll attack yourself with shame. Abuse takes you beyond not feeling good enough as it leads you into deep dark places of despair, isolation, and hopelessness. Like someone's addiction, you didn't cause the abuse, you cannot control the abuse or the abuser, and you certainly cannot cure the abuser of their anger.

Know that abuse of any kind in an intimate relationship qualifies as a betrayal. Such deception erodes your trust in your intimate partner. Your couple relationship is one place where you're meant to feel safe and secure. Anything less is unacceptable.

Exercise 9: What Feels Abusive?

1. Describe the ways (emotional, financial, neglect, physical, psychological, sexual, verbal) in which your partner's actions feel abusive.

2. Now describe an action you can take to protect yourself for each of the types of abuse you've listed.

Ending the cycle of abuse starts by first becoming aware that you are being abused or exploited. If you're reading and completing the exercises in this workbook, you are already working to break this cycle. If you feel threatened by your partner and feel unsafe, you must reach out for help. Make yourself safe—now!

Chapter 4

Grieving the Loss

Intimate betrayal is about loss. You have lost the relationship you thought you had, trusted, and counted on. You have forfeited the life you'd dreamed of, idealized, and hoped for, including:

- Your life as you knew it
- All the comforts of that life — physical, financial, social, and emotional
- Your couple relationship
- Your family dynamics
- Your sense of security
- Your trust in others
- Your confidence in yourself

And for all this, you grieve. Like any loss — death or non death — this impacting life event has no timeline for mourning. "Grieving takes the time it takes" (Dawn Cruchet, 2013).

In *Stillness Speaks* (2003), Eckhart Tolle explains the shift that happens when we experience a life-changing loss:

> *Whenever any kind of deep loss occurs in your life — such as a loss of possessions, your home, close relationship, or loss of your reputation, job, or physical abilities — something inside you dies. You feel diminished in your sense of who you are. There may also be a certain disorientation. "Without this ... who am I?" When a form that you had unconsciously identified with as part of yourself leaves you or dissolves, that can be extremely painful. It leaves a hole, so to speak, in the fabric of your existence.*

Molly said, "I felt profoundly lost in my loss. Being blindsided by Kevin's betrayal rocked the ground beneath my feet. I didn't know who I was after so many years of being part of a couple. What did I feel, want, need? Everything was up for questioning — even the parts of myself of which I was sure and confident."

Dawn Cruchet also explains that having experienced previous losses can compound grieving a current loss. We accumulate losses throughout our lives, so when faced with a major one, our grief can feel intense as we relive and mourn the painful reminders of those previous bereavements.

"Losing my mother when I was only twelve years old produced feelings of abandonment and aloneness, which I again faced in leaving Kevin. Ending our relationship reawakened these strong feelings, and ironically, I could have used Mom's support right then."

It took a full four years for Molly to mourn her loss of Kevin and their life together: "I can pinpoint the exact time the grieving finally lifted." Molly had accomplished her tough emotional work. "I felt good about how far I'd come through my healing."

Stages of Grieving

In her epic book, *On Death and Dying* (1997), Elisabeth Kübler-Ross explains the five stages of loss and grieving: denial, anger, bargaining, depression, and acceptance. The order of these five stages may interchange as you go back and forth between them as many times as necessary.

The loss of an intimate relationship through betrayal feels like the death of the alliance you once had or believed you had. Life losses qualify as non-death losses. They carry the same hallmarks. Let's look at the way these stages of grieving might unfold around intimate betrayal.

Denial

You learn about the deception and may refuse to believe it exists:

- How can he do this to me, to us, to our family?
- I don't believe/think that she has acted out sexually or betrayed my trust.
- He isn't that type of person.
- She'd never do such a thing!

The reality is that the sex addict leads a double life. Like a stage magician, the betrayer may practice smoke and mirrors—pointing at something about you over here while sexually acting out over there. The advantage to the addict is that while you're busy feeling shame about your shortcomings, you're too distracted to notice their dual life—and you don't learn about the betrayal.

You don't see the series of incidents that connect the dots. Your denial protects you from the harshness of reality. If something is too painful to deal with, you may mute it so that you don't feel the searing pain. That way, you don't have to deal with the full impact of the agony. You don't have to think about it. You dissociate.

At the extreme, dissociating is disconnecting from your own life, your consciousness, and your identity. It serves as a self-protective mechanism in response to trauma that may have occurred in an earlier dysfunctional relationship, perhaps in childhood. Dissociation becomes the default coping strategy that helps you get through subsequent recurring traumatic life events.

"Denial was my constant companion, helping me to cope with my early abuse," Molly recalls. "As a child, I didn't see my father's sexual compulsions, news of which later trickled through the family grapevine when I was older and after I'd experienced sex addiction in my partner."

Molly explained how, in retrospect, denial accompanied her in her first love relationship with a man named Ben. Molly was eighteen, and Ben was twenty-six: "I was naive about relationships and sex."

Two red flags occurred at different points. Ben had a temper that would flare suddenly. One time, in anger, he pinned Molly against a wall. "It was an isolated incident, so I thought nothing of it. Also, Ben's visiting aunt would stumble drunk into his bedroom and force herself on him sexually." She even visited Ben in his room one weekend while Molly slept soundly in the guest room across the hall. "When Ben told me that his aunt's drunken molestations occurred regularly, I merely took it in stride. After all, how could I feel threatened by an elderly auntie who just felt lonely?" Meanwhile, Ben's aunt was sexually preying upon Molly's innocent boyfriend. "Yet, a few years later, when Ben admitted that he'd just had a one-night stand with a friend, I ended our four-year relationship right then and there!"

Interestingly, Molly may not be the only one in denial about sex addiction. As of this writing, sex addiction doesn't even appear in the *Diagnostic and Statistical Manual of Mental Disorders* (DSM-5)! This renowned diagnostic tool published by the American Psychiatric Association is used by health care professionals to diagnose mental disorders.

Molly explains how denial obscured an early red flag when, within months of moving in with Kevin, she awoke one morning venomously angry and confrontational: "I had the vague feeling that Kevin had sexually violated me in my sleep. We'd had a glass of wine together before I went to bed alone, as usual. *Had I been drugged?* I'd wondered. I was distraught because here Kevin wouldn't come to bed with me, yet he'd somehow had sex with me while I slept!"

Eventually, Molly learned about Kevin's proclivity for somnophilia, a shocking foreshadowing of the kind of control he'd later exert over the unsuspecting victims he was ogling and viewing through binoculars and uncovered windows.

Denial played a pivotal role in Molly tolerating Kevin's porn watching on the television and computer. "I told myself that it was natural for men to view porn. Where did I learn to tolerate that nonsense? However, the behavior felt wholly uncomfortable for me because it crossed my boundary of what I value — as if Kevin's earlier sleep violation of me had not been enough of a boundary transgression!"

Still, Molly concedes that she didn't see Kevin's compulsive behavior as an addiction wreaking havoc in their life together, notably as it increased in frequency and intensity.

"I found it easier to blame myself for not looking attractive enough. Kevin would often tell me I was frumpy, that I'd gained weight. He'd make snide remarks about my wearing jogging pants while we were out shopping."

Given Molly's template of abuse, she didn't see that Kevin's disparaging comments about her appearance were outright bullying behavior. Denial once again blinded Molly: "I felt so unworthy that I didn't notice Kevin's escalating voyeuristic activities were no longer limited to viewing porn."

> Stop the self-blame. It only delays the decisive action that can help you heal.

Unequipped to deal with the impact of Kevin's addictions, Molly comforted herself with potato chips and chocolate bars.

Rachel's Story

Rachel was a stay-at-home mother of twins. She found herself shouldering the entire responsibility of running the household and taking care of their children. Her husband, Sam, wasn't available or present most of the time. When he was home, he'd zone out, like he was in his own private world.

A programmer with a reputable technology company by day, Sam would spend most of his off-hours in his attic office, completing coding projects for clients. Eventually, their marriage disintegrated, ending due to irreconcilable differences.

Years later, Rachel learned that Sam was in prison. He'd been found guilty of making and distributing online child pornography. She'd had no clue. Was this what Sam had been doing in his home office? Rachel hadn't seen the signs—or she'd dismissed Sam's behavior as related to his heavy workload. She even recalled thinking that maybe Sam was a workaholic.

***

Also crucial is acknowledging your sadness about your loss when you discover how painful intimate betrayal feels. Eckhart Tolle talks about self-victimization in the face of profound loss:

> *When this happens, don't deny or ignore the pain or sadness that you feel. Accept that it is there. Beware of your mind's tendency to construct a story around that loss in which you are assigned the role of victim. (2003)*

If you're blaming yourself for denying clues, put away the whacking stick. Stop the self-blame. It only delays the decisive action that can help you heal.

Anger

You're so angry that you see red! You may want to strike back and hurt the addict. Of course, you're enraged at having been so deceived. Molly related her intense feelings of anger: "I got angry—outraged. How could Kevin do this to our family and me when I trusted him and had invested so deeply in our life together?"

Possibly, you're also mad at yourself—for not seeing the clues, for trusting, for letting the betrayer get away with it. Feeling anger is a healthy response. Anger, like a burglar alarm, alerts you to danger: it tells you that someone has crossed your boundary.

What you do with your angry feelings is what matters:

- Avoid reacting in a way that could boomerang back to hurt you.
- Consider that sexual deviance is more about the addictive behavior than about the addict.
- Keep the focus on the action—the sexual acting out and its consequences.
- Consider that the betrayer may feel as helpless and powerless in the face of their sexual acting out as you do.

You aren't condoning or accepting or tolerating the behavior. Instead, you acknowledge the action for what it is and realize that the sexual acting out has nothing to do with you. It's not your fault. Not seeing the clues earlier is also not your fault.

A year after Molly left Kevin, while sorting family photos backed up onto her computer, she came across a series of disturbing images filed away in an unmarked folder. They were butt and frontal below-the-belt shots of a teenage girl clad in shorts. "Suddenly, a memory came flooding back to me, one I'd brushed off," Molly recalled the zip-lining activity with their daughter who, tethered to a cable, gleefully swung from tree to tree. Other families and children milled about on the ground. "I remember Kevin photographing our airborne child with his camera. Then I noticed him taking snapshots of a teenage girl standing under a tree. I immediately reprimanded him for taking pictures of someone he didn't know and without her permission. These were the shots I'd found stored on my computer."

At the time, Molly hadn't even clued into this form of 'upskirting' as sexual acting out. Subconsciously, however, she'd recognized Kevin's behavior as wrong, and asked him to stop.

Remember that addicts are incredibly skilled at hiding their compulsions. They're crafty. Even they may not be fully aware of the extent to which they're protecting their acting out from coming to light. The sex addict may be unaware that their behavior is hurting you. And if they are aware, they don't seem to care because addiction robs the addict of empathy. And the persistent denial of their partners helps sex addicts continue their behavior unobstructed.

Dr. Patrick Carnes explains addicts as having a brain disease that alters their perceptions. Active addicts have a distorted sense of their reality. And they certainly *do* distort ours!

Molly used her anger toward Kevin gainfully: "It fueled my departure. In fact, for the first time, for me who'd been the emotional barometer in this dysfunctional relationship, I had no words left to say. Plus, I chose not to engage in any further deliberation that might influence my decision."

Molly said she'd almost decided to give it yet another try with Kevin: "A remarkable instance occurred when Kevin told me we'd work things out this time. He almost had me convinced to turn around and sublet my newly rented apartment, which I was a month away from occupying."

Thinking about Molly's dilemma, I recalled something a friend of mine shared about the problem of leaving an addict: "It's hard to 'throw it all away' when you've invested so much in the relationship. It reminds me of a gambler who spends so much time and money playing a slot machine and is determined to keep pumping in coins, convinced that, with persistence, it will pay off."

Molly recounts how she'd said 'Yes' to Kevin: "I agreed that we'd try again and sat with my intense disappointment for a few hours. I'd so wanted to believe him and that the vision of a happy life together was still possible. I reprimanded myself. Then I reminded myself of the reason I was finally leaving Kevin."

Unlike all the other times, Molly wasn't feeling it in her gut: "My good sense prevailed." Molly resumed labeling her packed boxes: *Fragile. Handle with care. This side up.*

With valued support, Molly began to move forward with her own life and priorities: "I saw friends more often. I channeled my anger by immersing myself in creating my new life: packing, purchasing items for my new apartment, and concentrating on all activities related to me." Molly stopped cooking for Kevin. She no longer ate with him. She detached in all ways to facilitate the final severing of ties.

Something else: Molly's daughter didn't move in with her until a year later, opting instead to finish her senior year at a boarding school. For her part, Molly gained valuable space to learn about living by herself. She wanted no official ties with Kevin since her daughter was of legal age. "I financially contributed to my adult daughter directly, thus eliminating contact with Kevin as much as possible. I wanted a clean break. I didn't want to feel angry and resentful anymore. I wanted to quietly and privately do my healing work. I liked this newfound self-care. It became my new pattern."

Bargaining

You hope with all your heart that things will change. You may tell yourself messages like:

- "If only I were more: sexy, attractive, a better partner, homemaker, parent" (Fill in the blank), "maybe my partner would not sexually act out."
- "I will strive to be more …" (Fill in the blank), "and perhaps my partner will stop sexually acting out."
- "I will work harder on my relationship."

I call this 'enoughness.' The truth is you *are* enough. You did not cause your partner's sexual acting out. You cannot control or cure it by bargaining it away.

Molly explained, "I bargained a lot throughout the years of my relationship with Kevin when I thought I was dealing only with his excessive drinking. When I returned to our shared home after being locked out, I dedicated myself to completing the exercises in a self-help book about saving the couple relationship. We had agreed to discuss these exercises a few nights a week, and I'd share my discoveries with Kevin in the hope that he, too, would participate and work to save our steadily sinking ship."

It was futile having these talks after dinner while Kevin lubricated himself with wine. "He couldn't focus. He couldn't engage in the intimacy of the exercise. Instead, the discussion would again turn to his evangelizing about the ideals of distant spiritualist writers. These were not the talks of a couple working to save their relationship; they were the 'Oh, Enlightened One' talking down to 'the Inferior One' in the corner wearing the dunce cap! I felt frustrated and waylaid. Once again, I was bargaining to save the unsalvageable. After a few weeks of this, I gave up entirely."

So, when she discovered that Kevin was peeping in windows, this was the turning point for Molly. She realized that Kevin's behavior was far more severe: "I decided not to bargain anymore for change. 'I'm done!' I'd told Kevin."

Molly was indeed through. Although she still had no label for what she'd discovered, Molly couldn't unknow what she now knew. She'd unveiled Kevin's sex addiction, and this was Molly's cue to exit the relationship. Molly had hit bottom in her relationship with Kevin.

Depression

Someone's addiction has wreaked so much havoc in your life that you may feel defeated as you ask yourself:

- "How could my efforts to change the situation fail?"
- "Surely if I were more ..." (Fill in the blank), "my partner would stop this behavior, and everything would return to normal."

Once the gravity of the situation sinks in, you may feel profound sadness about your powerlessness to change your partner's sexual acting out. Being sad is not the same as depression. Depression is a deep state of melancholy and sadness. The American Psychiatric Association explains:

> *A common and serious medical illness that negatively affects how you feel, the way you think, and how you act. Fortunately, it is also treatable. Depression causes feelings of sadness and ... a loss of interest in activities once enjoyed. It can lead to a variety of emotional and physical problems and can decrease a person's ability to function at work and home.* (2018, online)

While grief can have some of the hallmarks of depression, such as intense sadness and withdrawal from usual activities, it's crucial to notice heightened feelings so severe that you:

- Lose interest in your regular activities
- Lose your appetite
- Have trouble sleeping
- Want to sleep all the time
- Cannot function well in your daily activities
- Feel panic attacks
- Feel general physical malaise
- Withdraw from others

The above characteristics signal that the sadness is more debilitating and may point to depression. You may need outside help to get through this. If sorrow is overtaking your life, consider consulting with a qualified psychologist or with your family doctor. Consider this because depression can result from post-traumatic stress disorder (PTSD), a psychological response to trauma. Realize that the shock of intimate betrayal can lead to depression. If left unchecked, depression risks becoming chronic and more challenging to deal with as time passes.

Acceptance

Moving toward integrating all the feelings, you are coming to terms with the intimate betrayal. You agree to face the situation and your new reality with all the tools in your toolkit.

> 66 My story is merely a story. It doesn't define me.

Acceptance doesn't mean condoning your partner's sexual acting out. Acceptance is the act of facing your situation with courage and willingness.

Dr. Camillo Zacchia, a psychologist and anxiety expert, talks about how we must deal with trauma: "Not only do we have to get over what happened, we have to get over the fear of it happening again." He explains that healing occurs when we learn to accept what's happened and acknowledge the situation for what it is. Dr. Zacchia quotes a client: "'You don't get over your loss. You learn to walk beside it.'" (October 19, 2016). He suggests writing your story out from beginning to end to help deal with your trauma.

Molly explained how she'd kept a journal over the years, documenting occurrences and her feelings about them. Now she wanted to write out the details of her discovery. Molly made daily journal writing a priority. "So I could log the process," she said.

Molly joined a breakup aftercare group where writing their narratives was the prime focus. Writing out her story was cathartic: "First, because I found my voice. Second, because in the telling, I released the pain of my narrative. I reclaimed my power and my authority. Now my story is merely that. It doesn't define me."

You will grieve the loss if you haven't already. There's no way around it. There's only going *through* the grieving. One day, you'll come to accept your impacting loss.

Molly recalled noticing the veil of grief lift: "It was early autumn, three years after I'd left Kevin and my former life. I could finally look back without feeling a heavy sadness. I felt at ease in my life and well in my skin." Molly was ready to put her healing to the test: "I even felt ready to contemplate a new love relationship."

Exercise 10: My Story

Tell your story, writing it out from beginning to end.

Grief Work

Working through grief involves first taking stock of where you're at in your grieving process, then taking steps—when ready—to look at what resources you have at your disposal to continue through to the end of your grief work. Although you may not feel strong because you're grappling with the trauma of betrayal, you are, in fact, strong *because* you are dealing with this very challenging life event. See where you *are* strong and leverage that to go the distance through your grieving.

Mobilizing My Resources

Perhaps you've been relying on your partner to meet your needs. They've let you down horribly. To count on an active addict for support and comfort is much like milking a cow and expecting orange juice. You may feel very angry about this: first, because you trusted, and second, because you held certain expectations of your partner, along with a vision of your life together.

At the various stages of loss and grieving, where possible, you need to take stock of your resources—inner, physical, financial, and social. You must learn what your needs are and then find ways to help yourself meet those needs. You may have subjugated your needs to those of the sex addict, especially if you're caught up in the chaos of worry and confusion. It's time to return to basics.

What specific self-care activities might you have been postponing? Perhaps start by planning a special outing or meeting with a friend. As you progress, this could mean preparing for your financial well-being and putting some money aside.

Molly needed to trust that she could indeed provide for herself financially: "All along, I'd been supporting my family through my contract work. I paid my fair share of the bills. There were times when Kevin was unemployed. I'd add on another work contract to even the deficit. Imagine, here I was, doubting my proven capacity to live by myself!"

On Christmas Eve, one month after Molly left Kevin, she recalls standing next to the lemons in a large grocery store when her cell phone rang—the phone she regularly texted on despite Kevin's criticism about her 'inability to learn.'

It was Kevin. He told Molly that she'd made a mistake in renting an apartment. Why not stay with her brother?

Molly said, "The underlying message sounded like 'I want to see you fail so you'll be back.'" And she told Kevin clearly, "I make my own decisions about where I live and whether or not I choose to rent." Then she added, "If it were up to you, I'd be living in a cardboard box under a bridge!" With that, Molly hung up. *Happy holidays to you!* She was especially proud she'd reclaimed her power; the symbolism of the lemons didn't escape her.

Molly affirmed, "I was now the one controlling my finances. I learned I could provide for myself and my daughter and have money left over!"

Social engagement was critical for Molly. Friends and family rallied around her, offering their support. "These were people from whom I'd slowly isolated as the chaos of dealing with Kevin's addictions became all-consuming. I learned what they thought about Kevin and how they'd held back their comments, respectfully allowing me to come to my own conclusions."

One family member told Molly that there was an energy about Kevin that had felt uncomfortable. A friend used the phrase 'creeped out' based on conversations with Kevin. "If they'd shared this with me at the time, I wouldn't have listened because I was in my full-blown denial," admitted Molly.

Now with her new tribe, her collective supported and sustained Molly through the hard work of healing that lay ahead: "There were no 'I told you so's,' just welcome, love, and belonging."

During this challenging time, we must also learn to reach out to others for the help we need. Whereas we may have isolated ourselves while dealing with the problem of our intimate partner's sexual acting out, now we can draw upon the help, love, and support of others. Knowing the limits of our personal resources is critical so that we can mobilize what we need and from where/whom.

This next exercise is one that you may revisit and revise during your grieving because as you advance through the stages, you will feel stronger. Your early responses to the following questions may look very different from the answers you give later in the process.

Exercise 11: My Resources

1. What external resources are available to me? How can I reach out?
2. How can I mobilize any resources available to me to take care of my:
   - Body and health—physical and mental
   - Physical safety and security in my environment

- Money and finances
- Social and belonging needs
- Need for love and companionship
- Inner and emotional life
- Spiritual well-being

As you move through the stages of loss and grieving, know that you have a wealth of resources—inner and outer—that are available to help you through this profoundly life-altering event. If you do the work, you'll come out stronger. Just give it time.

Chapter 5

A Holistic Approach to Healing

For complete healing to take place, it is crucial that you simultaneously work on your body, mind, and self because your entire being has been affected by intimate betrayal on each of these levels. Feeling good about ourselves—our sense of self-esteem—directly relates to our self-worth as we care for ourselves holistically. When we experience intimate betrayal, we need to heal body, mind, and self to heal our whole person.

'Enoughness' and Self-Worth

There will always be people and situations that test our feelings of 'enoughness.' Our greatest challenges have the potential to make us stronger once we face and overcome them—even if we have to go through hell and hit bottom before finally taking back our power. Brené Brown, in her book, *Braving the Wilderness* (2019), talks about not negotiating our self-worth with other people:

> *Don't walk through the world looking for evidence that you don't belong because you will always find it. Don't walk through the world looking for evidence that you're not enough because you will always find it. Our worth and our belonging are not negotiated with other people. We carry those inside of our hearts. I will not negotiate who I am. If I negotiate who I am for you, I may fit in with you, but I no longer belong to myself.* (MarieTV, online, September 2017)

Brown also explains that when we negotiate our self-worth with another person, we are betraying ourselves.

Body, Mind, and Self

Prioritizing our self-worth so we can find our way back to feeling that we are enough exactly as we are, is crucial to healing from intimate betrayal. We can do this by caring for ourselves on all levels of body, mind, and self. Below are some key activities for holistic healing of body, mind, and self. A more comprehensive list appears toward the end of this chapter.

Body

The body holds pain, not only at the physical level but also at a deep cellular or root level. Scientists have realized that memories reside in our cells and not just in the brain:

> *Over the last 50 years and especially the last 15, experts have verified that the source of your symptoms of pain and anxiety is usually not located in your body or even in your environment. The source is located in the unseen issues of your unconscious*

and subconscious mind, or what science calls "cellular memory." (Lloyd, 2018)

Canadian singer/songwriter Shania Twain explains in her memoir, *From This Moment On,* that she lost her singing voice after her husband and her best friend betrayed her through their affair. This infidelity broke up Twain's marriage and business partnership and destroyed the friendship. Impacted profoundly by this double betrayal, Twain later explained this event as "a trigger crisis" in her interview with Oprah Winfrey. Emotional hurt can ultimately manifest collateral damage in the body.

The body holds the pain of memories. When the body heals on a deep cellular level, the effects manifest at a physical level. Take, for instance, people who've experienced rape. Later, even in a loving relationship, touching or attempting penetration can cause the body to clamp up and retreat instinctively.

> Adopt a somatic practice. The idea is to try a physical activity you usually would not do, something that gets you out of your body's comfort zone while moving.

Molly had wondered if it's common for women who'd experienced intimate betrayal to cry profoundly after every orgasm: "I'd sob guttural, wracking cries like an animal in pain. Was it my body's reaction to the trauma — or was it my body's way to heal?"

It's crucial to release the pain that may cause an intense body reaction to recover in your core. Find a body practice — Tai chi, dance, running, yoga, power walking, working out, etc. — to which you are willing to commit and do regularly. The idea is to try a physical activity you usually would not do, something that gets you out of your body's comfort zone while moving.

Molly experimented with meditation movement, a form of dance and improvisation in response to diverse types of music, rhythms, and beats: "This practice had me moving meditatively, animated by a skilled instructor who safely helped me to explore the space and relationships around me in a playful way. I became aware of my breath, my feelings, and my emotions as these expressed themselves through a variety of free-flowing movements."

Practicing this dance grounded Molly in her body as her feet connected her core to solid ground: "I had to focus and stay present to the experience. It ignited my creativity, my connection, and my community with others," Molly recalled.

Dance helped Molly to integrate body, mind, and self and heal her pain at a deep cellular level. "It especially helped me work on my trust of others." Those tender feet, once stabbed by sharp splinters, became instruments of connection to Molly's core, propelling the healing movements that freed hidden layers of her self.

Molly undoubtedly accomplished some fancy footwork in taking charge of her holistic healing!

Exercise 12: Adopt a Somatic Practice

What body practice (physical activity) appeals to you? Why?
Find one and commit to it.

> ### Exercise 13: Mirror Mirror
>
> Stand in front of a large mirror and answer the following questions:
> 1. What do I see when I look at *me* in the mirror?
> 2. Who do I see?
> 3. Do I see what I like or mostly what I dislike?
> 4. What do I see that I like or love about my body?
> 5. How can I see what I like and truly appreciate these parts of me?
> 6. What positive self-talk can I use when I look at *me* in the mirror?

Another crucial change in habit for Molly was to cease consuming alcohol: "I decided to no longer have a relationship with a substance that had wreaked so much havoc in my life. So, I stopped all social drinking." Molly gained a remarkable boost in clarity and confidence.

Mind

The mind and psyche can hold onto painful memories. We may not even be conscious of these memories, hidden from the mind, that can dramatically affect our everyday behavior.

Post-Traumatic Stress Disorder

Intimate betrayal can be a highly traumatic experience. It can shake you to your core. As with any trauma, you may be experiencing post-traumatic stress disorder or PTSD: "Post-traumatic stress disorder (PTSD) is a mental health condition that's triggered by a terrifying event—either experiencing it or witnessing it. Symptoms may include flashbacks, nightmares, and severe anxiety, as well as uncontrollable thoughts about the event" (Mayo Clinic, 2018).

Pauline, a woman in her seventies, is still triggered by thoughts of her husband's betrayal. She shared her feelings decades after her experience: "This is a murder of the soul. Healing may take years. It may never really heal because just recalling it can make it alive again."

Groundbreaking new research from Northwestern University identified a specific brain mechanism that can conceal traumatic fear-related or state-dependent memories in the brain—and how these are triggered:

> *State-dependent memories can be positive or negative. In many cases, traumatic or stressful experiences are buried from consciousness as a protective mechanism. Inadvertent or unexpected stimuli linked to the state-dependent memory can trigger acute flashbacks that are often the hallmark of post-traumatic stress disorder (PTSD). Researchers believe this process is a neural defense mechanism designed to protect the psyche of an individual from being incapacitated by fear-inducing memories. However, if suppressed memories aren't coaxed out of hiding and brought to the surface, they often lead to debilitating psychological problems, such as anxiety, depression, PTSD, or dissociative disorders.* (Bergland, 2015, online)

Sometimes PTSD can manifest in an intense body response when a painful flashback occurs, resulting in trembling, shaking, sobbing, sweating, or becoming cold and freezing up. PTSD requires the intervention of a qualified therapist.

It is common to have difficulty adjusting and coping when you experience a traumatic event, and it doesn't always lead to PTSD. Over time, by taking good care of yourself, you will likely begin to feel better. However, if the symptoms worsen or last for months or even years, or if you find you can't function properly in your everyday life, then you may have PTSD. If you think this is your situation, please consult your family doctor or a qualified therapist (See the section on depression above).

Let's look at some ways you can help your mind to process and deal with the shock of intimate betrayal.

Therapy

Also called the talking cure, therapy can help you cope with the intimate betrayal by your sex-addicted partner. A qualified therapist or counselor can help you talk through your feelings about your intimate partner's betrayal. He/She can help you to work through the early patterning that has you stuck in non-productive, self-defeating, codependent behaviors. A therapist can also help you discover your blind spots, triggers, and emotional obstacles that keep you stuck.

Therapy helps you:
1. Get in touch with and cope with your feelings
2. Solve problems by adopting new perspectives
3. Change behavior patterns
4. Learn new ways of dealing in your interpersonal relationships

"Working with a psychologist was extremely helpful for me," recounted Molly. "It helped me deal with my fears about leaving

Kevin. The support of my pull-no-punches therapist challenged me to keep moving forward in my resolve to safely exit the relationship and to break the pattern of abuse for once and for all. I attended group therapy sessions with other abused women who were also dealing with addicted partners. And I attended individual therapy sessions. This intense work was critical for healing the legacy of abuse that I'd been living."

Through therapy, you can:

1. Realize small break-throughs
2. Learn about your strengths
3. Look at the past to make changes in the present
4. Learn new skills for dealing with life challenges
5. Achieve catharsis

"A huge learning for me was how to enact and exercise my own choices and boundaries in a relationship. Whereas before I was caught up in people-pleasing, therapy helped reinforce new strategies for getting my needs respected and met." Molly said.

Coaching

Coaching can help you set the wheels in motion to move forward with your life. Coaching is a trust relationship whereby you work collaboratively with a life coach to:

- Define what matters most to achieve your goals
- Gain clarity
- Stay accountable while exploring some of the challenges that may be holding you back

- Help you reach, stretch, change, and grow in any direction you desire based on a plan of action

A coach supports you through the process of finding the answers that genuinely lie within you. They do this by listening to you, helping you explore your successes, strengths, and resources, sharing ideas and offering suggestions, and helping you develop a plan of action.

Although coaching is not therapy, it can be therapeutic.

Other practical ways are available to quiet the mind and stop the negative mental chatter that loops over and over in the wake of discovering your partner's deception.

Meditation

The act of meditating—being still, closing your eyes, and focusing on your breath—can help stop or slow the hamster wheel spinning in your head. Yes, it can be difficult to still your mind and silence your thoughts.

Start small, first aiming for two or five minutes of meditation. When other thoughts arise, acknowledge them, turn your focus back to your breath, and concentrate on breathing through your nose. Be gentle with yourself. Meditation is a practice. It takes time to find your resting place. The key is to practice regularly. The conscious stilling of your mind opens space for healing.

Having said this, some individuals effectively still their minds by washing the dishes, making the bed, woodworking, painting, or going for a quiet walk in the fresh air. There are many ways to rest the mind. Find one that best suits you.

> **EXERCISE 14: TWO-MINUTE MEDITATION**

Find a short online meditation (there are many) to download to your computer, phone, or MP3 player. Carve out some time to listen and still your mind, which may be speeding to process your thoughts and feelings about your reality. Note how you feel after this exercise. Did it center you? Again, it takes practice to meditate. It's normal for many thoughts to rush through your mind. Acknowledge them and come back to your focus.

Reading and Studying

It's helpful to read memoir accounts of others who've experienced intimate betrayal and learn about addiction in general. See Recommended Resources at the end of this book for suggestions. You can also do a keyword search online to find more resources. When facing a life transition, some people return to school or studies, either taking a single course or a whole program. Sometimes these studies help ease this life transition.

You'll recall that I'd wanted to leverage what I learned about myself through my life transition to help others. I decided to study life coaching. My actual process of training to become a life coach felt like being ripped open by a can opener at times because my innermost self was exposed. I began to rethink my oppression.

Through the activities of this program—mainly individual coaching—I was invited to review my way of being and my inner patterning, which had steered me to repeated relationships with abusive addicts. I'd bowed to their expert authority about *me*. They hijacked and then re-scripted my story. I allowed them to add more chilling chapters. I needed to stop this behavior if I was to change and grow forward.

Molly found her place, too, when she returned to school to study counseling. Her learning impacted her life transition: "I challenged and questioned everything I thought I knew about myself—the little nine-year-old girl who, while her gun-wielding father threatened to blow her mother away, faced the tough decision about whether to stay and guard Mom or run to ask the neighbor to call the police. I'd stood on our unfinished cement balcony wringing my hands in crippling indecision. That immobile, fixed cement slab would come to symbolize every situation of inertness in which I found myself. That petrified platform symbolized my feelings of 'stuckness,' particularly during the many false starts I'd experienced around leaving Kevin earlier."

Molly also challenged her victim mentality. She peeled back that label: "My psychic scar, the blemish I thought everyone could see as my mind kept playing over and over the shameful facts of the betrayal, was only visible to me." Molly dared herself to change her story from victim to victorious. "I came to realize on a strong intuitive level that I was exactly *enough*. I'd established a new stable and sturdy platform. I became my rock!"

Exercise 15: Learn About Sex Addiction

Using the Internet, type in the keywords 'intimate betrayal' and 'sex addiction'. Sift through the online articles, forums, and information websites (See Websites under Recommended Resources at the end of this book). Learn about the disease of sex addiction so that you can be informed. Knowledge is power; information helps us make clear decisions.

Self

Unbeknownst to us, the self has a journey. A hurt self must mend. Healing can inspire a more in-depth look at the legacy handed to us. Maybe our destiny is not a place where we end up, but instead, the process by which we get there. There are lovely surprises along the way.

It seems that Molly was traveling toward an inner peace—a journey that took most of her childhood and half of her adult life. In its own time, her self spoke its truth to Molly from within—from a place of inner knowing, despite the pattern she'd acquired as a frightened child with a dangerous father. Molly's abused spirit sought and found healing: "Today, unbound, my self flows and grows. I've found good, healthy reciprocal relationships. Now, I connect with a collective of people with whom I feel safe and can be myself."

Positive affirmations are powerful for helping the self heal. Saying these can change the often-negative mental self-talk. Repeat positive words and phrases many times during a day or while meditating. When you repeat affirmations, you reprogram your mind with positive thoughts that can shape your new patterns. One I particularly like is by Charles F. Haanel: "I am whole, perfect, strong, powerful, loving, harmonious, and happy" (2017).

According to Australian writer Bevan Lee, the words 'I am,' followed by whatever you put after them, have the power to shape your reality. What we tell ourselves, we believe. We can use powerful words to define our new narrative.

Exercise 16: How I Am Enough

List how you are enough:

Exercise 17: I AM...

As you fall asleep at night, recite 'I am ...' followed by positive adjectives and qualities that describe you:

- I am gentle.
- I am competent.
- I am beautiful.
- I am loving.
- I am loved.
- I am _____.
- (Keep going.)

Trust

Our trust in ourselves erodes when we live with someone else's crazy-making behavior. We second-guess ourselves. We may be so off-balance and out of touch with our needs and wants that we feel insecure and incompetent. We do not trust ourselves. We need to relearn how to trust ourselves and trust what comes up for us in the moment so that we can begin to forge healthy boundaries—with ourselves and in our relationships with others.

 Trusting comes when your internal validation system kicks in.

Sometimes you need to allow information to flow to and around you. You need only acknowledge what you see, hear, smell, taste, touch, or intuit through your senses. You feel something at the gut level; this refers to trusting your intuition. Trusting comes when your internal validation system kicks in. You receive the information, process it, and determine your perception of it. Often this happens subconsciously. You are unaware of yourself working on data. At a certain point, you begin to intuit some vital information.

Clara's Story

Recently, after giving a talk about my personal story at a conference, a beautiful young woman I'll call Clara, approached me, tentatively at first. She told me that what I'd said about dealing with a partner's sex addiction made her wonder if she, too, had been facing this in her boyfriend with whom she'd lived and had recently left. Clara felt objectified, like her appearance, her sensuality, even her aging, were scrutinized continuously by Chad. Clara was puzzling about whether Chad's behavior was indeed sex addiction. At that moment, I felt like I was bearing witness to Clara's intuition kicking in. I observed her final confirmation that she'd made the right decision for herself.

***

Imagine that you're clenching five small objects in your hand, your fist closed tightly so as not to drop any of these items. You notice that your fingers tense to curl into your palm, as you cradle the items. Depending on how tight your grip, it can feel uncomfortable. Your knuckles turn white. You grasp tightly—you mustn't drop the pieces, or you risk losing them. When you clutch too tightly onto your worries about someone else's actions, you hold onto your pain around the betrayal, and you hold onto an unhealthy relationship that is not serving your needs.

EXERCISE 18: LETTING GO—ALLOWING AND TRUSTING

Take one or two small unbreakable items into your hand and hold these as described above.

- How does it feel to hold these objects tightly?
- What do you notice about your hand?

Loosen your grip, notice your hand, and then release these objects.

- What happens to the objects?
- How do you feel?
- How do you feel about what happens to the objects?

Can you allow yourself to do this with problems, worries, concerns, and issues? How? What is the worst that can happen if you release them?

A huge part of healing is trusting. We're so used to doubting what comes up for us because of the crazy-making aspects of dealing with our partner's sex addiction that caused us to second-guess ourselves. As you heal, you grow. You believe what comes up for you—be it a feeling, a boundary, or a knowing. You learn to listen to and trust this inner voice, *also known as intuition,* that is telling you what you know to be right for you at that moment. And you learn to test out your intuition through clear communication with others.

Molly gave an example of trusting her inner voice when she decided that she'd no longer have a relationship with her abusive father: "I'd gone to his home to talk with him about all the hurts he'd inflicted and was still inflicting on me. I'd wanted to work things out with him and move past the hurts to have an honest and healthy relationship with my father." Although he was rooted in his drinking behavior, her father honored Molly's request to remain sober for their talk.

However, Molly's father didn't react well to her explicit 'I message' where she focused on her feelings. "I told him how his actions had hurt me and that I wanted it to stop by telling him: 'I felt abused when you drank and were violent with me as a young child. This made me feel sad and unworthy. I'm still having challenges with you as an adult because when you drink, you act mean and say nasty remarks. I need you to stop treating me this way. Or I cannot have a relationship with you,'" Molly said.

His only retort was to strike out at my motherhood. He told me that my child was 'a little animal.'"

Molly left knowing that she'd no longer tolerate her father's toxic venom: "He wouldn't see me again, and he forfeited any opportunity to watch my 'little animal' grow up." In twenty years, Molly has never looked back: "Whenever I was tempted to mend fences a few times over the years, I'd quickly remind myself that I'd only get sucked back into my father's unaddressed dysfunction and gross abuse. Leaving Kevin closed the loop."

Another example of Molly trusting her inner knowing occurred not long after she was living on her own. She was driving home and discovered that a car seemed to be taking every turn she made. "It felt too close for my comfort. I suspected that someone was following me. Rather than scold myself as paranoid, I drove past my building and kept turning quickly onto side streets while looking in my rear-view mirror to see if I'd lost my possible follower. Once I felt reassured, I drove home." Molly trusted herself and did what she needed to feel safe and secure.

On yet another occasion, while shopping at a local department store, a man quickly brushed past Molly, making full-body contact: "I was shocked and speechless!" Instead of questioning herself, Molly knew what had just happened. It had a name. What she'd experienced was frotteurism, a form of sex addiction. The perpetrator rushed off before she could react: "I exited the store. Today I'd report it. After all, stores have cameras," said a confident Molly. "I'll never doubt my instincts. I am my barometer. And because of this, I am also my best protector."

Exercise 19: Trusting My Inner Voice

Think about a recent situation in which you trusted your inner voice or your inner knowing. Write in your journal:

1. What was the occurrence?
2. What did I think or know about that situation?
3. How did I honor my knowing?

Exercise 20: Trusting My Inner Knowing

Journal about your day:

- What was one moment when a feeling, boundary, or a knowing arose?
- How did you receive it?
- Pay attention to your reaction to your inner knowing. How did you act upon it when you first recognized your feelings about a situation?
- Did you censor yourself? If so, why?
- What did you learn about yourself?

Holistic Healing Activities and Practices

BODY

ACTIVITIES	IMPACTS
1. Doing physical movement, sports activities, walking 2. Esthetic treatments (facial, manicure, pedicure) 3. Getting reflexology, Reiki, bodywork (massage, reconnective healing), salt therapy treatments, etc. 4. Meditating – sitting or moving 5. Going to a health spa 6. Doing relaxation exercises (Total Body Relaxation) 7. Writing/journaling 8. Artistically expressing yourself via drawing, painting, singing, dancing, etc. 9. Decluttering your space 10. Breaking a habit or quitting something	✓ Gives energy ✓ Relaxes muscles and releases tension (stress) ✓ Gets blood and oxygen flowing ✓ Promotes heart health and general well-being ✓ Produces endorphins ✓ Equalizes serotonin levels ✓ Contributes to physical fitness ✓ Boosts body confidence ✓ Improves self-image ✓ Increases metabolism and helps digestion and elimination of waste and body toxins ✓ Helps you to get unstuck

MIND

ACTIVITIES	IMPACTS
1. Reading/studying 2. Talking with someone 3. Meditating – sitting or moving 4. Doing relaxation exercises (Total Body Relaxation) 5. Attending psychological therapy/counseling—individual, couple, or group 6. Working with a life coach 7. Attending a support group 8. Repeating positive affirmations 9. Engaging in a hobby/leisure activity 10. Writing/journaling 11. Attending an event: play, concert, festival, seeing a film 12. Artistically expressing yourself via drawing, painting, singing, dancing, etc. 13. Engaging in religious/spiritual practices 14. Breaking a habit or quitting something 15. Decluttering your space	✓ Calms—refocuses your attention and stops the spinning of the hamster wheel in your head ✓ Helps you feel not so alone or isolated ✓ Engages you in life ✓ Promotes learning and self-growth ✓ Fosters self and other awareness ✓ Boosts self-confidence ✓ Helps you to get unstuck

SELF

ACTIVITIES	IMPACTS
1. Attending a support group 2. Attending psychological therapy/counseling—individual, couple, or group 3. Working with a life coach 4. Meditating – sitting or moving 5. Attending wellness retreats, going to a health spa 6. Repeating positive affirmations 7. Writing/journaling 8. Engaging in religious/spiritual practices 9. Artistically expressing yourself via drawing, painting, singing, dancing, etc. 10. Breaking a habit or quitting something 11. Decluttering your space 12. Developing a new positive habit	✓ Calms—refocuses your attention and stops the spinning of the hamster wheel in your head ✓ Enables relaxation ✓ Promotes community ✓ Creates a spiritual connection (with a higher power) ✓ Fosters self-confidence ✓ Counters codependency ✓ Boosts self-esteem ✓ Puts the focus on you, your priorities, your life, and your goals ✓ Helps you to get unstuck

Declutter Your Way to Becoming Unstuck

The topic of clutter deserves a special mention. Clutter refers to excess items or things we keep but don't need or use. Excess items can form piles, occupy too many surfaces, and clog up our living space. Clutter can also obstruct our path. Sometimes we collect and hold onto things in our attempt to preserve memories. Or we don't discard junk and let it build up around us. The result is clutter. External clutter may reflect our internal mess or feelings of disarray.

Decluttering can be a helpful activity because doing so frees up physical space; it can also free up mental space. When we have too many items cluttering our environment, we may feel stuck. We can't move. While possessions hold memories, they also goad us to conserve what we no longer need, want, or use. Sometimes holding onto these things means clinging to the past. Hoarding is at the extreme end of this spectrum, and may point to an underlying issue that could benefit from a therapeutic intervention.

When we declutter, we change our energy. We rid ourselves of what no longer serves us, and we practice the healing

 Decluttering helps us reclaim our authentic self. Letting go of the past clears space for the life we want.

art of letting go. We remove both physical and psychological obstacles from our path. We live our lives more fully and with intention. When we remove clutter and become organized, we develop focus, reduce stress, and boost creativity. It opens our living space and our headspace. Decluttering helps us reclaim our authentic self. Releasing the past clears space for the life we want.

Molly began decluttering their home the year before she'd been locked out by Kevin. Bags and boxes were filled and deposited in the car for donation as Molly emptied shelves, drawers, and cupboards. "Although the house wasn't cluttered, I'd felt this need to lighten up my space. I felt excited to be putting order into my life! A close family member observed that I was paving the way for a significant change!"

Molly lightened the energy around her. She purged what she no longer needed, wanted, or enjoyed. Entirely unbeknownst to Molly at the time, decluttering was likely a precursor to purging her unhealthy couple relationship.

Annabelle's Story

When Annabelle was in her late fifties, she looked around her home and saw piles everywhere. An avid garage sale-goer, Annabelle couldn't pass up a good deal. She was down to one uncluttered sitting room in the small home she shared with husband Greg. Greg was never there, so Annabelle felt no pressure. Suddenly Annabelle asked herself why Greg was never home. But she knew. Annabelle had overheard the late-night cell phone calls. She'd felt Greg leaving their bed when he thought Annabelle was asleep for the night. Annabelle awoke early to find the bed empty and later heard myriad excuses from Greg about his having to go back to the office. Annabelle made a life-changing decision to remove all the stuff—to clear away the clutter obscuring the life she was living. She tossed and donated items until the house was clean and orderly. Greg was gone yet again. Annabelle decided to file for divorce: "Garbage in. Garbage out."

***

> **EXERCISE 21: ADOPT A REGULAR HOLISTIC HEALING PRACTICE**

Review the list of activities above. Can you think of any other practices not mentioned here? Now, start by committing to one regular exercise from each category of body, mind, and self. Integrate these practices into your life. To help with this, ask yourself these questions:

1. What one activity am I willing to commit to doing this week?
2. Is there someone with whom I might do this activity?
3. What might get in the way of doing my chosen activity?
4. How can I anticipate and plan to overcome that obstacle?

These exercises are not a substitute for therapy with a qualified therapist specializing in this type of trauma. Instead, they can serve as a complement to treatment. You can heal in body, mind, and self by releasing yourself in as many ways as possible.

Chapter 6

Stopping and Starting

We may find ourselves stopping and starting many times. The very nature of making a significant life change might entail pausing periodically. When we pause, we aren't necessarily standing still; instead, we are processing. Like studying for a test, when we take a break and do something else, our mind is still working on the material.

Guilt and Resentment

Guilt and resentment are two bedfellows that keep us anchored in dysfunction, both with ourselves and with another person. These can be the biggest hurdles to making a significant life change because they affect our decision-making about what's best for us, they usurp our confidence, and they rob us of our positive self-esteem.

Guilt is the gift that keeps on giving and is unproductive. Often, guilt has been instilled in us from our early learning in our relationships with significant others. Guilt is based on 'shoulds.' Shoulds are usually based on the perceived or explicitly communicated expectations of others. For example, if I feel guilty about taking care of my needs, I may think that doing so means that I'm selfish or uncaring. Whose story is that? Often, we've been told this story by other people who question us in an attempt to control us.

You'll recall Molly's slab or precipice, which for her, represented feeling frozen in place and therefore stopping. "There were times when it all felt so overwhelming that I wanted to nap simply to stop the over-thinking," Molly said. "It was always with me. There were these thoughts about how could I have done things differently. I was chastising myself for not doing enough or being enough. Eventually, I ceased my constant self-criticism. It had suited my addicts that I walked with my head down and my eyes closed tightly shut. I started to lift my head, open my eyes wide, and acknowledge both my intelligence and my vision."

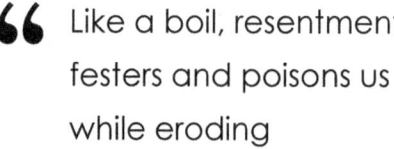

You may have heard the expression, "Resentment is like drinking poison and expecting the other person to die." We suffer when we resent someone else. I recall an Oprah Winfrey show where she talked about her resentment and anger toward someone. She explained how one day, from a distance, she saw this person coming out of a department store in New York City, bags in hand, and chatting and laughing with a friend. Here she was feeling angry and resentful while this person was living her life, having fun, and had no clue!

> Like a boil, resentment festers and poisons us while eroding the relationship.

Resentment is a poisonous pill that releases slowly. We harbor resentment, actively nourishing it with that negative mental self-talk tape we play over and over again in our head. Like a boil, resentment festers and poisons us while eroding the relationship. It is no wonder that we find ourselves physically ill when we carry around long-standing resentments toward someone else.

When someone does or says something that we don't like or that makes us feel uncomfortable, we can practice detachment. When our partner engages in sexual acting out, we can let it go. Rather than swallow the poison of resentment, we can tell ourself that we don't own the other person's words or behaviors—they don't belong to us. Instead of dying inside, we give it up. In doing so, we can let the other person take responsibility for something that was never ours. We are now free to go shopping, laugh with a friend, or do another activity that gives us pleasure and boosts our self-esteem.

Stephanie's Story

Stephanie's partner Gwen is a love addict. Gwen regularly starts new relationships with other women. Stephanie feels much guilt, and she resents Gwen. Each time Gwen disappears for a few days chasing another love relationship, Stephanie feels despair and believes it's her fault. She can't seem to let go of the guilt she feels about not feeling good enough. She finally decides to leave Gwen, and Gwen begs for a second chance. Stephanie plunges into more guilt over her decision to end this dysfunctional relationship. "I needed to let go of my guilt so I could let go of Gwen and our unhealthy relationship," Stephanie admitted. She left, and Gwen went into treatment for her sex addiction. "We're still in touch, but now I'm taking care of my own life and priorities," Stephanie said.

***

No one can make us feel guilty or resentful without our permission. We have the power to stop ourselves, put away the whacking stick, and practice gentle patience with ourselves, with the other, and with situations over which we have no control.

We must break the old patterns of guilt and resentment as these have caused us to accept the unacceptable from ourselves and others. We need to let go of guilt and resentment so that we can let go of our unhealthy attachment to the sex addict's behavior, which we do not own. In this way, we can begin to implement the changes necessary for prioritizing our own lives and engage in self-care vital for moving forward.

Let's reconsider the concepts of stopping and starting as these relate to self-care:

Stop	Start
Accepting the behavior	Accepting what is
Condoning the behavior	Acknowledging the behavior
Blindly trusting the betrayer	Learning to trust me
Begging to be loved	Loving myself, beginning with the small details
Returning to the situation that hurt me	Detaching and letting go
Tolerating abuse	Setting clear, healthy boundaries
Bargaining for a second chance	Choosing to give a second chance only if I want to and with conditions, agreements, and consequences in place that respect my healthy boundaries
Holding myself hostage	Freeing myself from the bonds of guilt about, resentment of, and attachment to the other person's unacceptable behavior
Forgetting	Learning

Consider letting go of the pain, the hurt, the worry, and the anguish—all the negative aspects of intimate betrayal you are holding onto that may be keeping you tethered to relationship chaos. Acknowledge that you have learned something from this experience so that you can attract a better, healthier experience for yourself—either alone or with a healthy partner. You can free yourself from invisible chains binding you to the sex addict and their actions.

Molly said her journey around stopping and starting felt bumpy at first: "I alternated between not thinking about Kevin's deception, to overanalyzing it. I felt overwhelmed by the thought of letting go of the fact that Kevin had deeply hurt me. I'd read this quote that resonated with me spiritually: 'I think there are two kinds of forgiveness, the kind that when you forgive, you're also giving them another chance, or the kind where you forgive, but move on without them. Use them both wisely. —S. B.'"

Molly took two actions around starting. First, she did a meditation in which she imagined Kevin holding a balloon filled with all the hurts his actions had inflicted. "I envisioned him floating upward and away with the balloon despite that every fiber of my being wanted to take a large pin and prick that sucker mid-flight! After that meditation, I felt light and relieved."

Molly explained that although she'd moved on, she needed to start living well—fully and unconditionally. "I needed to let go of the fact that I'd tolerated the unacceptable for so long. I needed to release the reality that I'd blocked real joy while I stayed stuck. I wanted to let go of the fact that I'd immersed myself in these protracted life lessons well past the learning curve. Ultimately, I stopped criticizing myself for being human."

One day, a gentle relief—so subtle—filled Molly's heart. "I felt the heavy burden of grief lift. I'd moved on and felt ready to welcome new experiences. Refocusing away from Kevin and toward my new life took time, but this ushered in new meaning for me. It was worth all the hard work of making profound changes. And I was confident the changes would stick."

Life Tests

Life will test you along the way to see if you've learned the lessons of your pain. You may find yourself meeting someone or encountering a situation where you're facing yet again, shades of your past hurts or challenges. Life presents you with an opportunity to show yourself that you've healed. Think of it as a do-over.

Molly experienced that very reality a few years into her healing. "I joined a study group as part of my university work and was de- Life will test you along the way to see if you've learned the lessons of your pain.

lighted to find a new friend, another woman, Marcia, with whom I had so much in common. We enjoyed the same interests. We also shared the bond of having been recently divorced. Our friendship grew, and we spent much time together doing activities, dinners, and even taking a vacation together. Slowly, I introduced Marcia to my long-standing friends, and she became part of my friend group," Molly said. After awhile, Molly observed Marcia's affinity for drinking wine. Molly began to feel uneasy in her relationship with Marcia, and couldn't quite figure out what was bothering her. "I just knew that I didn't feel safe with Marcia," Molly recalled.

Another friend of Molly's noticed how Marcia would sling verbal barbs at Molly, and she told Molly about her observations. "I'd felt it, but I still had this blind spot. I eventually recognized that I was being tested to see if I'd learned my lesson from having dealt with Kevin's emotional abuse." Molly put her friendship with Marcia on ice after one particularly challenging situation that arose between them. "I was still in my heavy healing work from the intimate betrayal," she explained. "But this time, it didn't take me as long to discover the betrayal in this friendship."

Molly's learning curve was indeed shorter. Life had presented her with another abusive relationship to test that she'd learned her lesson. She didn't commit energy toward fixing this friendship. Rather than wonder why she'd attracted yet another abuser, Molly congratulated herself: "I saw the situation for what it was before the relationship could drag me down," said Molly.

Exercise 22: My Stopping Work

Design a 'letting go' affirmation. It could be something like:

- I let go of blaming myself for missing the clues of my partner's sexual acting out.
- I let go of blaming myself for believing the lies my partner told me about his or her whereabouts/actions.
- I let go of feeling guilty about my angry reactions when I didn't know what was going on.
- I let go of resenting my partner for being emotionally unavailable to me.

Go ahead—your turn.

- I let go of blaming myself for ...
- I let go of my resentment about...
- I let go of feeling guilty about...

Exercise 23: My Starting Work

There is no pressure to turn away from the person who has deceived you. Take a moment to reflect on what it might *look* and *feel* like to turn away from the intimate betrayal you suffered.

- Write a few words or draw a picture of turning *to* your own life.

Has life tested you yet?

- Write about a person or situation that has provided you with an opportunity to test your healing.

Now let's gently segue into moving forward.

Chapter 7

Moving Forward

How do you move forward from intimate betrayal? By reading this book, you've already begun.

Transition

Imagine a wall, and your back is against it. There's nowhere else to go but to face the change before you. When I've stood with my back against the hard, un-moving wall of what I knew I must do to change my life, I wished that the wall would move—just a little bit. *Give me more time, more space, more energy, and make me enough so the wall will budge, and I won't have to!*

> 66 Change often happens when our back is against the wall. And still, we cling to the hope that the wall will move.

In her song "Change," Tracy Chapman aptly describes how a situation must deteriorate before we hit bottom and seek change. I heard this song at a women's wellness retreat. Its power to connect with my most deep-rooted fears about loss and regret helped me name them. I suggest that you listen to and read the lyrics of this song. Does the message resonate with you?

Change often happens when our back is against the wall. And still, we cling to the hope that the wall will move.

For Molly, the most challenging aspect of going forward was chipping through what felt like an insurmountable wall of a life transition. "Something had changed. I needed to adapt to a new reality." Molly found herself on a shifting landscape in unchartered territory. "I even questioned those areas in which I felt competent and thrived. I knew I had to rethink my life. My resistance to redesigning it was intense. It's so scary to change!"

Exercise 24: What If...?

Writing or drawing in your notebook or talking with a trusted friend, consider these questions:
- What is my greatest hope?
- Can I stay with my partner and rebuild our relationship?
- If we stay together, can I trust my partner again?
- Will I be able to love and trust another partner again?
- What does love/a healthy relationship look like?
- Am I willing to let go of the past to embrace a happier future?
- If I leave, is there someone else out there for me?

- Will I attract someone else who is addicted to sex or who will betray my trust?
- What kind of life will I have now?
- What are the highest priorities in *my* life?

Fear

As a child, watching her mother's very life threatened by her father, Molly stood frozen on the unfinished concrete slab that was the front balcony of their home. It was Molly's first precipice. "Torn between wanting to run for help as my mother begged me to do and feeling unable to disobey my violent father, I felt paralyzed with fear. Much later, as an adult, knowing I needed to leave Kevin, I froze on my second precipice. Fearing the unknown, I didn't move. Once again, fear kept me cemented in place."

Imagine standing on a precipice, about to jump into the unknown. You know that you are adequately geared up like a parachutist who's practiced and ready. You freeze because you fear that unknown. So, you do not jump. Fear keeps you bolted in place.

Fear kept Molly tied to the dysfunction of an intimate relationship, and ultimately, it prevented her from acting. "I dared not move from fear's grip or change anything. *How will I take care of myself? How can I survive this? What do I do now? What if …?*"

These are all fear-based questions that Molly asked herself, as I once did, and that perhaps you may be asking yourself. An acronym for FEAR is 'false evidence appearing real.' Old false messages kept Molly stuck. "I couldn't move forward for so many years because I believed that I couldn't take care of myself. That was untrue. I was merely afraid!"

It's normal to feel dread when facing the unknown, especially a change so significant that it seems strange and surreal. When you recognize fear is harnessing you, then you can do something. You can take baby steps. You can begin to thaw. Slowly, you can move past your anxiety. It's a process, much like grieving. And like mourning, it takes the time it takes.

Initially, it might feel like a grueling slog through the sludge of a challenging life transition. You trudge through all the muck. You come to discover so much beauty and joy on the other side of change. You may even feel relief and wonder why you didn't make the journey sooner. No regrets here—everything occurs in its right time.

Exercise 25: If I Weren't Afraid, I Would...

Reflect on and answer the following through writing, talking, drawing, or dancing:

1. Of what am I *most* afraid?
2. How is this fear keeping me stuck in my situation?
3. What is one small step I could take today that would make a difference?
4. How can I take that step? What do I need?

Working Through

As you grieve and take stock of your life and your losses, you are creating a new space for yourself. You are now prioritizing your needs. You are refocusing from the sex addict to your own life and your well-being. A critical aspect of creating a space for yourself is understanding your boundaries or limits. In other words, we must know where we begin and end apart from our sex-addicted partner with whom we may feel enmeshed (Refer to Codependency in Chapter 2).

Healthy Boundaries

Healthy boundaries are the rules we set for ourselves and how we honor ourselves: our feelings, our needs, our wants, our values, and our safety and well-being (physical and emotional) within ourselves and in our relationships with other people.

There are three kinds of boundaries:

1. **Rigid** - keeping others at a distance (emotionally, physically), avoiding intimacy, being detached and guarded, and having difficulty reaching out for help.

2. **Porous** - getting too involved with other people and their problems, over-sharing information, having difficulty saying 'No,' being dependent on the opinions of other people, and tolerating abuse.

3. **Healthy** - not compromising our values for other people, knowing and communicating our limits, wants, needs, sharing personal information appropriately, and can say and accept another's 'No.'

Personal boundaries fall into six categories:

1. **Physical - our personal space and touch**, which someone violates when they invade our personal space or makes unwanted physical advances or touches us when we

don't want them to. Healthy physical boundaries involve being aware of appropriate touch and giving and receiving consent.

2. **Intellectual - our thoughts and ideas**, which someone violates when they put down or dismiss our ideas or thoughts. Healthy intellectual boundaries refer to knowing what is appropriate to discuss in different social and professional situations, how, and concerning confidentiality.

3. **Emotional - our feelings**, which someone violates when they belittle, criticize or put us down or otherwise invalidates our feelings. Also, when we over-share without properly developing a relationship with someone, we breach our own emotional boundaries.

4. **Sexual - the emotional, intellectual, and physical aspects of sexuality**, which someone violates with unwanted touch, sexual comments, and pressure to engage in sexual acts or in uncomfortable sexual acts. Healthy sexual boundaries hinge on clear communication between partners about wants and desires and mutual understanding regarding limits.

5. **Material - our money and possessions**, which someone violates when they take away or dispose of our possessions or pressures us to lend or give money. Enacting healthy material boundaries means setting limits on what money and possessions we will share and with whom.

6. **Time - how we use our time**, which someone violates when they demand too much of our time or otherwise controls or takes up our time. Healthy time boundaries mean prioritizing our time for each aspect of our work, life, and relationships.

Many of these boundaries may have been transgressed by the sex addict and through our dealing with the chaos of their compulsive sexual behavior. If you feel numbed out from your trauma, you may have difficulty even knowing what you think, need, want, or value. You learned to subjugate your needs to those of your sex-addicted partner. You come second or third in your own life. This destructive habit may have eroded your importance without you being aware.

Establishing healthy boundaries means more than merely saying 'No.' The process involves first becoming aware of what you need to feel safe, loved, and respected in your couple relationship. You acknowledge by letting yourself feel that need without guilting or shaming yourself for it (or allowing anyone else to). You then express your needs to your partner, and finally, you honor your truth.

> How to Establish Healthy Boundaries:
>
> 1. Know what I feel, need, or want
> 2. Acknowledge without judging myself
> 3. Express what I feel, need, or want
> 4. Honor or stick to my boundary without guilt

Molly learned about healthy boundaries: "Kevin disregarded my emotional boundaries by putting me down. He also disrespected my intellectual boundaries by discounting my ideas. Through his evening rituals he violated my time boundaries," Molly said.

"I often expected Kevin, sick in his disease, to validate me. I wanted love from someone absent from his own life. I wanted him to be present to mine. That's like waiting at the locked front door while my partner drinks wine and polishes his binoculars! I sought partnership from an addict too weak to be a partner." Like Molly's father, Kevin, who was not well, couldn't be present to Molly. "I kept hoping Kevin would change, just as I'd hoped my father would, too. Clinging to hope kept me stuck."

Molly knew she needed to feel safe and secure in her relationship with Kevin, but he could not give that to her: "I would call Kevin out on his rude remarks to me. He often had a justification. I was quick to shoulder the blame. Then I realized that it wasn't me. There was something else going on."

When Molly finally realized the sad reality of Kevin's abuse, along with his sexual acting out, she told Kevin that she could no longer be in a relationship with him—and she didn't back down from her decision to sever ties.

Let's recap the steps involved in establishing healthy boundaries:

1. **Awareness**—knowing what you feel, need, want, and value now (Knowing your truth)

2. **Acknowledging**—allowing those feelings without judging yourself (Accepting your truth)

3. **Expressing**—sharing your feelings, needs, desires, and values (Expressing your truth)

4. **Honoring**—sticking to your boundary without backing down out of discomfort, guilt, shame, keeping the peace, etc. (Honoring your truth)

Helping Versus Enabling

Helping relates to healthy boundaries; enabling is the opposite. Helping is the act of being in the service of someone. It arises from a healthy interdependence. Helping allows me to say, "Yes, I can do this for you or with you" when doing so doesn't compromise my time, energy, or values. Helping is when I give according to my limits. So, when faced with a request, I give myself a choice. I might say, "I cannot do this, but this is what I can do."

Enabling is doing for your partner what they can and should do for themselves. Enabling someone crosses a boundary. It's damaging to both the addict and you. It causes you to regard another adult as helpless, incompetent, and without any personal authority over their own life. Treating your partner this way is disrespectful and demeaning. It's not your job to rescue your sex-addicted partner from the social, financial, legal, or other consequences of their sexual acting out.

Establishing boundaries was critical to Molly's recovery. Regular attendance at her support group helped Molly to understand and express her healthy limits.

For example, two years after Molly left Kevin, the police called her. "They asked me to come in for an interview because they caught Kevin peeping into a neighbor's window. As I drove to the station, I considered a few facts. Kevin's most recent acting out had not had anything to do with my cooking skills, my physical appearance, my wardrobe choices, or my ability to learn new things. I was nowhere around, and Kevin's illicit, unlawful voyeuristic activities had carried on, independent of me. That day, I answered all the investigator's questions truthfully."

"When Kevin learned that I'd spoken with the police, he called me. I heard his outraged accusations. I should have covered for him. How dare I divulge his private secrets to the law by sharing damaging information! How did this happen? Why did I betray him? In one fell swoop, Kevin completely boomeranged the responsibility back to me: It was my fault. I was the the bad guy, *once again*."

Sound familiar? Suddenly, Kevin turned the table. He, the hapless victim of Molly's big mouth, was being watched by the police.

"I quickly stood up for myself during that call. I told Kevin that I wouldn't lie or cover up for him." Molly hung up the phone, firm in her decision that she'd never again enable Kevin's immoral behavior. She recognized that it's dishonoring on her part to usurp Kevin's adult responsibilities. "I wondered if my truth-telling at the police station that day shocked Kevin into recovery," said Molly.

Exercise 26: One Single Boundary

Reflect on and write about an accomplishment in successfully respecting one small boundary of your own this week:

1. Describe the situation and people involved.
2. How did the other person react to your setting a boundary?
3. How will having set that boundary affect your life?

Getting clear is one way to get healthy. Applying certain fundamental principles can guide your thinking and your life to help you stay clear about your limits and your values. This next exercise helps you to implement these ideas, one at a time, to continue healing your whole self.

Exercise 27: Working Through

Writing or drawing in your journal, or talking it over with someone, express your thoughts or feelings about the following:

- **Honesty:** How am I now being honest with myself? With others? With the sex addict?
- **Hope:** What is my most significant concern for myself in the face of this situation?
- **Trust:** Where is my trust rooted?
- **Courage:** What do I need to develop the courage to face?
- **Integrity (Honor):** How can I best honor myself right now?
- **Willingness:** What habit am I willing to change?
- **Humility:** For what am I most grateful?
- **Love:** How do I best love myself right now? How do I best love others?
- **Justice:** What quality of life do I deserve?
- **Perseverance:** With what do I need to stay on track?
- **Spirituality:** What reflective practice suits me?
- **Service:** How can I best volunteer for my recovery right now?

To get started, ask yourself:
1. What do these ideas mean to me?
2. How can I practice these in my daily life?
3. How can I practice these during a moment of crisis or challenge?

4. How can I apply these ideas in my relationship with my intimate partner who has betrayed me?

Molly worked through the fact that, along with the addictions, she'd been dealing with years of compounded abuse from her family of origin and in her intimate couple relationships. She read Beverly Engel's *The Emotionally Abusive Relationship: How to Stop Being Abused and How to Stop Abusing* (2002). A renowned therapist specializing in abuse, Engel explores the hallmark patterns of low self-worth, the cycle of leaving and returning, and repeating those destructive patterns with new partners.

Diligently doing the work of these exercises helped Molly question familiar patterns. "When I completed the exercises and reread the many pages, I could see that my unhealthy early patterns had colluded in establishing my present unhappiness." She'd been a prisoner of her first patterns. "It felt empowering and powerful to create a new order in my life and watch it all unfold!"

Molly began to change her patterns. "I started to overcome the challenges involved in breaking the cycle of abuse. These exercises inspired me to turn my story into a healing, self-help journey."

Check-In

So, here you find yourself a little more than halfway through the activities in this workbook. Let's do a check-in:

- Are these exercises helping you gain clarity?
- If yes, how?
- If not, what do you sense you need?

The next four exercises aim to establish your plan to move forward with your life in a positive way. They can also help you know what to look for in a healthy partner.

Exercise 28: What I will not Tolerate in an Intimate Relationship

Express your healthy boundaries. Go ahead and list them all!

Exercise 29: What I Don't Want in an Intimate Partner

The idea is to get clear about what you will not tolerate in an intimate partner. Be exhaustive in your list.

Exercise 30: What I Want in an Intimate Partner

Go ahead and make your wish list. Know that you are attracting healthy people, relationships, and events into your life.

Exercise 31: How I Am Moving Forward

List how you are moving forward with your life.

The Family System

Although this workbook is about you and the impacts of intimate betrayal, there are also interpersonal relationships and social dynamics to consider because you are part of a system of family and friends that may include:

- Young or older dependent or adult children living at home
- Adult children living on their own
- Extended family members such as siblings, in-laws, parents, and other relatives
- Friends/couple friends

A considerable stressor might be who, what, when, and how to tell. We are as sick as our secrets. Secrets may have played a large part in the dysfunctional dynamic in our family of origin. However, there is a crucial difference between what is secret and what is private. You are the only one to decide what you'd like to disclose, how, when, and to whom.

While intimate betrayal is between you and your partner, there's still the matter of handling what your children and other significant people in your life need to know, especially when the family configuration changes. Some questions about how to navigate this reality with all the parties above include:

- What do I tell them?
- How much should I tell and to whom?
- When do I tell others?
- Who should be the one to tell?
- Will I/we be judged?
- What if they don't speak to me/us again?
- What if people found out and make me/us/our children feel like outcasts?
- How will I cope with my feelings of embarrassment and humiliation?

There is no one right answer to disclosing to others your discovery of intimate betrayal. You have a right to your privacy and your boundaries. Over-sharing with the wrong people or sharing with people with whom you are not close doesn't help to maintain healthy boundaries. Trust your inner voice.

When Molly first learned about Kevin's voyeuristic violations, she suspected that he also targeted a neighbor, Jeanne, and her adolescent daughters: "I carefully approached my neighbor to warn her and give her a chance to protect her family." This conversation was enlightening because it validated their various observations about Kevin, glaring clues they'd both missed. "I told Jeanne that I'd found his binoculars outside. And she told me about finding a misplaced deck chair pulled up to their stairless back patio door. Now Jeanne wondered if Kevin had used this chair to watch her sleep on the sofa when her husband worked night shifts."

Although they'd never know the extent to which Kevin breached the family's privacy, Molly and Jeanne noted the evidence of Kevin's voyeurism. "Jeanne said she'd now be more vigilant about closing the window shades," Molly recalled.

As for telling close friends and family, Molly didn't hold back: "I knew that people close to me would understand and support me in my decision to leave Kevin. I also knew that to heal, I would need to divulge the secret that, for so long, had eluded me. I shared with close relatives and friends, and finally, in my support group. The understanding I received was overwhelming and touching. When I was able to share my story with men in my support group, their compassion felt particularly healing."

Be aware that not everyone will have a healthy response to your disclosure about your intimate partner's sex addiction. Don't be hurt or shocked by it. Instead, understand

> **Be prepared to walk away from the kinds of conversations that leave you feeling empty and blamed.**

that they are unwitting participants in the time-honored conspiracy of silence, the one that says: *Don't talk. Don't trust. Don't feel.* They do not yet have the maturity nor the awareness about sex addiction to compassionately respond to your pain. Groomed to silence from an early age, many people cannot acknowledge, let alone empathize with your suffering. Be prepared to meet it:

- Some may victim-blame or shame or question how you did not see this. (How blind could you be?)
- Others may wonder why you will not stand by your partner during their 'tough time' of having been discovered.
- Some may question your decision to stay.

- Some may avoid the discussion altogether because it's too uncomfortable for them.

You can't win with such people. You don't need to defend yourself to friends and family who are not supportive of you. Recognize that their reactions may stem from their misguided perceptions, insecurities, and experiences. Be prepared to walk away from the kinds of conversations that leave you feeling empty and blamed. Asserting your boundaries remains critical. Be judicious when choosing to share with others. Select only those whose maturity you trust.

Ken's Story

Ken, from Chapter 1, experienced a double stigma when he shared his story about being betrayed by Jules. First, Ken found himself alone with the fallout of Jules's betrayal, which caused his medical diagnosis of HIV. Second, friends of both he and Jules ostracized Ken. Some people judged him harshly, blaming Ken's lifestyle for his predicament, despite that he and Jules were in what he'd thought was a caring, committed relationship. He felt devastated and alone. Connecting with a support group for gay partners of sex addicts proved to be a lifeline for Ken.

***

Telling your children is another essential step. Your children will be as shocked about their parent's sexual acting out as you were. When speaking with them:

1. Keep the conversation age-appropriate.
2. Share what is only necessary for your children to know.

3. Reassure your children that none of what is happening is their fault.

Perhaps you want to disclose more details to your child out of fear of being disbelieved or disowned by that child if they side with their sex-addicted parent. It is indeed a fine line. Use caution here. Consider a consultation with a psychologist or social worker.

Sharing the delicate details of your partner's sex addiction with your child is highly inappropriate, especially if you are angry and want to strike out at your partner or you are feeling so isolated that you turn to your child as a confidant. Your child is not responsible for your emotional well-being. Sharing intimate sexual details with your child is, in fact, emotional sexual abuse, and it violates their safety and security. It can burden them, causing worry, stress, and outright psychological trauma for your child. They may be too young to grasp the situation. Remember that your child's experience of your partner (their parent) and their sexual acting out may not even resemble yours.

"In her terrible isolation, my mother turned to me as her confidante, although we were both on the receiving end of my father's violent outbursts." Molly's mother shared details about her husband's sexual abuse that Molly's ten-year-old mind couldn't grasp, which added tremendous stress to Molly's already burdensome reality. "I felt powerless to help my mother through her hell."

Even adult children would rather forgo knowing all the details of their parents' sex life and its inherent struggles. Interestingly, most kids think that their parents don't even have sex (Go figure!). Instead, share with a trusted close adult friend or extended family member. Seek professional counseling and adult support because, at some point, you will probably need to work through your trauma about the intimate betrayal with a professional who is equipped to help you.

Important: In cases where there has been a breach of your child's physical, emotional/psychological, or sexual safety and well-being by your partner, you must take direct action to protect your child. Engage with a therapist, social worker, or mediator. Reach out for this help immediately to assist your child in dealing with their trauma.

About two years after Molly left, Kevin committed another violation, one involving Jeanne and her family. He'd been suspected of peeping into their basement window to invasively ogle Jeanne's daughter and her boyfriend. The police tracked Kevin's boot prints in the fresh snow, which led to knee impressions at the basement window. When confronted, Kevin minimized this terrible, invasive offense by saying that perhaps, just maybe, he'd gotten a little bit too close to the neighbor's basement window while putting out the garbage.

For Molly, learning about Kevin's repeated sexual acting out was a huge trigger (Read more about triggers below), one she thought she'd already overcome because she was no longer in a relationship with him. Moreover, Kevin's severe wrongdoing raised the issue of what to tell her daughter, now living with Molly. The notion that her daughter might haphazardly learn about the shocking situation and suffer trauma convinced Molly that an immediate talk was necessary. Jeanne and Molly sat down with Molly's daughter. "We stuck to the bare facts. We explained that we felt Kevin needed help. We did not judge, blame, or shame my daughter about her father."

Exercise 32: Honest Conversations

1. Decide who you want to tell (Make a list).
2. How will you tell them (Alone, together)?
3. What exactly will you say?

Should I Stay—Or Should I go?

Deciding whether to stay or leave is a tough decision you may make and rethink many times. Listen to the valuable messages your gut tells you. Sit with it. Steep yourself in the truth of your body's signals. Consider not making a significant decision around staying or leaving for one year. Use this time to detach with love and observe yourself and your partner. Notice what you see. Ask yourself questions and communicate with your partner, honestly and openly.

What qualifies me to tell you to stay or leave? Nothing. I remain impartial here, bringing you stories that might inform your own. As mentioned earlier, this workbook aims to give you the space to reflect and decide for yourself what action you will take. When you are honest with yourself, and you listen, your own words will speak your truth to you. You need only be open and willing to hear them.

Molly explained her high tolerance levels: "For many years, each time I'd reach a breaking point, I chose to stay. I would try harder, more, and for longer. I'd be patient. I was loyal to a fault."

Molly happened to overhear her daughter's comment about her mother's pathological loyalty. "A teenage cousin asked my daughter if I'd leave this time, referring to having been locked out of Kevin's home. My daughter replied, 'She never does.' My daughter's comment profoundly impacted me. I had to look at what my actions were saying loud and clear. Was I teaching my child about putting up with abuse? Did I want to model that I'd continue tolerating Kevin's abuse? Like my beloved mother before me, my behavior spoke louder than words to my observant child. I decided it was time to choose actions that would testify to my strength and self-respect, respect that I so wanted my daughter to hold as her own high standard," Molly said.

"I finally chose to leave Kevin to break the cycle and heal this all-too-familiar pattern of relating ingrained since childhood. I was no longer willing to continue the chaotic boomeranging that had me leave and return several times in the past. I needed to get out. I needed to save myself."

> Intimacy is a great act of vulnerability that penetrates our existential aloneness because it allows us to connect with another.

Intimacy

Intimacy is the physical, emotional, and spiritual connection we have with ourselves and with another person. Usually, people associate intimacy with sex, but intimacy is so much more and equates with letting someone see, hear, touch, fully know, and cherish us. Intimacy or 'into me you see' is a great act of vulnerability that penetrates our existential aloneness because it allows us to connect with another, forging and fostering trust through:

- Closeness
- Belonging
- Togetherness
- Attachment
- Rapport
- Confidentiality
- Companionship
- Affection
- Understanding
- Mutual respect

We are born alone, and we die alone. Everything we do in between is our attempt to connect and feel connected with others. Understanding the role vulnerability plays in how and why we connect is key to understanding intimacy. Brené Brown, in *Daring Greatly* (2012), explains how vulnerability relates to connection:

> *Connection is why we're here; it's what gives purpose and meaning to our lives. The power that connection holds in our lives was confirmed when the main concern about connection emerged as the fear of disconnection; the fear that something we have done or failed to do, something about who we are or where we come from, has made us unlovable and unworthy of connection.*

Intimacy allows us to be our most authentic self. The hallmarks of intimacy include:

- **Communication** - openly exchanging and listening

- **Boundaries** - setting healthy limits to get our needs and wants met
- **Honesty** - transparency in thought and action
- **Shared values** - those non-negotiable principles we hold that help us live according to what is most important to us
- **Building trust** - key for establishing and maintaining our bond based on confidence in ourselves, in the other, and in our relationship

While sex with another person is cast as intimate, sexual intimacy is only one aspect of a healthy couple relationship. Sex is a by-product of connection as we establish and maintain a bond with our partner. Earlier, we saw how the sex addict might be having lots of sex, but not engaging in real intimacy. Sex addicts have difficulty connecting—to themselves and to others. So they fill that void with sex. They have turned to sex (and possibly other substances) for intimacy and comfort rather than to their partner.

> We are born alone, and we die alone. Everything we do in between is our attempt to connect and feel connected with others.

When our partner sexually acts out, whether we become aware of it suddenly or slowly over time, we experience the harmful effects on our intimacy as a couple. Communication breaks down. An atmosphere of negativity and resentment surrounds our exchanges which often entail nagging, pleading, begging, and threatening. Fun and spontaneity suffer. Fun for the addict depends on being in their substance-induced state, while the spontaneity of being out of control in dealing with chaos has ruled for the partner.

Men and women experience connection differently: arousal happens for men as they use sex to connect emotionally, and women need that emotional connection to get aroused sexually (Gray, 2001). Nevertheless, sex with the addict may feel physically pleasurable but leaves us feeling empty and humiliated.

Honesty and transparency are forfeited as the addict protects their compulsion. Our emotions constantly change: we alternate between withdrawal and intensity. We may find ourselves withholding love, affection, and attention to avoid getting hurt by the addict's actions, yet again. We may be easily triggered to anger. And sometimes we merely feel numb.

Our core values are tested over and over again in the face of each episode of our partner's sexual acting out. The addict transgresses their boundaries by their inability to say 'No' to their sexual acting out, which transgresses our boundaries. We either become rigid in our boundaries or so porous as to barely have any in place (all or nothing) as we deal with the chaos.

Despite our hope, we lose faith in our partner, in the relationship, and faith that things will get better. Our couple and our life become unbalanced as the pain of disappointment and disillusionment invades every aspect of our lives.

All this betrays our trust and ruptures our sense of connection with our partner. We feel isolated and rejected. We don't feel safe. Here we've made ourselves vulnerable; then we feel hurt by our partner's sexual acting out—actions that may leave us questioning ourselves and our lovableness and worthiness. We fear disconnection and loss. Hence, the reality of intimate betrayal.

If we are to move past the hurt and the fear to recovery, we must rebuild trust. This is the tricky part. First, we must learn to trust ourselves, and establish an intimate relationship with ourselves. Then we can decide how we want to place our trust in and be intimate with another.

So, while I'm not telling you to stay in or end your couple relationship, I am advocating that you get clear about the reasons you would stay with or leave your sex-addicted partner. Only you know the specific circumstances of your relationship, family, and what is worth salvaging. Only you can decide what *you* need. The next exercises in this chapter aim to facilitate your decision by helping you get clear.

Staying—Now What?

Perhaps you've decided to stay because you and your partner love each other, and with the best intentions, want to work on your couple relationship. All the activities and reflection exercises in this workbook are even more vital. You must stay on track with you. Let's reiterate this: *You must keep on track with you.* Remember, you're rebuilding shattered trust—trust that your partner must earn again. Confidence takes time to rebuild. First, be gentle with yourself. Then you can be gentle (but firm) with your partner.

EXERCISE 33: STAYING

The following is a truth-telling activity. Reflect on these questions if you decide to stay:

- What are my reasons for staying?
- What are my hopes for my future with my partner?

- Are these hopes based on ideals, past attempts, shared history, or on a shared vision?
- Is my partner in this with me, wholly and entirely?
- What expectations and agreements are now clear to both my partner and me?
- What new boundaries do I now have in place with my partner?
- What could make me change my mind about staying?
- Where do I see myself one year from now? Three years from now?
- Where do I see us, as a couple, one year from now? Three years from now?
- What support do I/we have?

Follow these essential tips if you both decide to work together on your relationship:

1. Be realistic and honest with yourself and with each other about your expectations and intentions.

2. Continue working on you: your boundaries, your priorities, your needs, your life, your interests, your self-love, your self-worth, and your other family relationships and friendships.

3. Resist the temptation to harbor a grudge or hold your partner's past over their head—avoid bringing up the issue during unrelated arguments.

4. If your partner is in recovery, the dedication and intensity involved may feel like a new addiction. They must work their program diligently. You may feel left out at times.

Therefore, your focus on your recovery is essential. Work your recovery as diligently!

5. Be aware of your triggers and the emotional roller coaster. Work on your recovery, especially when emotions run high.

6. Take space and give space. Be conscious of your hypervigilance. Learn to tame it. Recognize any sensitivity you may feel as being about you and not about your partner (See items #3 and #4 above).

7. Find a leisure activity or hobby that belongs exclusively to you. Practice it regularly (Refer to Holistic Healing Activities and Practices in Chapter 5).

8. Date your partner again. It's all new. You must take time to rebuild trust. Time alone as a couple, dating and having fun together, can help this process of re-establishing a connection.

9. Restore the foundation of your relationship before engaging again sexually with your partner. Don't rush sex with your partner (See #5 above).

10. Be prepared to reassure your partner that you love them and the efforts they are making.

11. Hold regular check-ins involving honest dialogue with your partner about your shared goals, your areas of concern, and your life together.

12. Appreciate, live, and love your 'enoughness' in every aspect of your life. You ARE enough.

Hailey and Rob's Story

When Hailey decided to stay with Rob, she felt the weight of so much work ahead. Her husband was one of the lucky ones. To stay out of jail for his criminal sexual acting out, which involved rubbing up against and showing himself naked to unsuspecting women, Rob had to follow a court-mandated recovery program, which ultimately brought him to his knees.

You will find no better poster person for recovery than Rob. He attends regular support group meetings, speaks with his mentor every day, and stays accountable to Hailey in all ways (time, money, his whereabouts, and he does regular check-ins about these). Rob had wholly betrayed Hailey's trust. Not uncommonly, she feels disheartened by the rigorous demands of Rob's sexual sobriety because he's often at support meetings or helping other sex addicts through their crises.

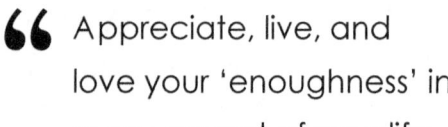

> Appreciate, live, and love your 'enoughness' in every aspect of your life.

Hailey regularly feels triggered by the fact that Rob still needs to leave suddenly, but now it's for sound reasons: to attend his support group if he feels triggered or to help a newcomer. She often needs to remind herself that she, too, has a place to go with her feelings as she attends a support group for partners of sex addicts. Hailey stays grounded in her own life, recovery, and healing from the devastating effects of intimate betrayal by diligently working on her recovery.

***

Leaving—What's Next?

You're clear about your decision to leave—or as clear as you can be. I once asked a divorced friend how she knew it was time to end her relationship. She said that one day she woke up and just knew. She assured me that I would know. The thing is, once you know something, you cannot *unknow* it. And going against that decision will not sit right with you. The many flashes of self-doubt don't make leaving any easier. Remain aware of these signals as they arise. Acknowledge them—and then let them go.

"Seeing my packed boxes lining the hallway, I'd rethink my decision and daily question my resolve. It was the hardest action to take: to move forward and leave, especially with constant, unremitting chatter in my head, coupled with Kevin's desperate pleas," said Molly.

The three months between Molly signing the lease on her new apartment and her scheduled moving date were long and sad. "While I felt fearful of the unknown, part of me felt excited by the prospect of this new opportunity!"

Earlier, we talked about the resources you need to access to prioritize yourself and your life. You've worked through that piece. You've reaffirmed yourself. You feel confident in your decision to leave. Let's walk together through this step once again—even if you've already taken it.

EXERCISE 34: LEAVING

If you've already left, answer these questions from your perspective at the time. If not, then use the following questions to understand *your* process of ending your relationship:

1. How do (did) I know the time to leave my relationship?
2. What could make me change my mind?
3. What challenges might I face? How will I overcome them?
4. What supports do I have (family, friends, community, resources)?
5. What am I most looking forward to about this next step in my journey?

You leave, and your journey begins. "A dear friend had told me that one day I'd be sitting on my sofa in my new home and it would hit me that I'd been delivered," Molly recounted her experience. "It wasn't the move, nor the army of friends who mobilized to get me from Kevin's house into my new home, but the aftermath. After the pizza boxes were put away and friends left with the promise to return for visits, I sat on my sofa and took it all in — the scope of what I'd just done: I'd left Kevin, my life, and the comfort of all I'd known for the unknown and a chance at happiness. I had to trust that I was where I was exactly meant to be."

Triggers

Whether you stay or leave, healing involves dealing with the triggers you experience because of being betrayed by your sex-addicted partner. A trigger occurs when you feel threatened by an event or situation that elicits an emotional reaction. Compounded by your fears and insecurities, your response stems from your perceptions (correct or incorrect). Remember that you cannot control or cure your partner's triggers to act out sexually.

You can, however, install healthy boundaries to help you navigate your intimate relationship. You can become aware of your triggers. For example, you might feel triggered when your partner takes a phone call in private or suddenly closes a computer window when you enter the room. You can even feel triggered by events such as a movie or a news report.

Helena's Story

When Helena decided to stay with Adam, who had a severe sex addiction involving pornography, she kept her appearance neutral. She wore very little make-up and avoided dressing in revealing clothing or suggestive outfits, not wanting to trigger Adam around visual cues that might cause him to act out sexually. Adam, for his part, wasn't physically attracted to Helena's appearance. He'd view digital sexual imagery using his cell phone. This action would trigger Helena, who felt frustrated that here she was doing her utmost to avoid triggering Adam with her appearance, and still, he was sexually acting out.

***

In a news documentary (SBS, 2018) about the double lives of sex-addicted partners, one woman explains how she feels triggered when recalling the pornographic images of female child victims she'd seen on her husband's computer. While this woman doesn't believe she will ever stop feeling triggered, she wants to eliminate the feelings of trauma that arise each time she *is* triggered.

If your triggers result in feelings of trauma, consider seeking counseling with a qualified therapist.

What we tell ourselves can influence the way we view and how we feel about a situation. Mental self-talk plays a vital role. Try to minimize the negative self-talk and ramp up the positive self-talk. Keep an open mind—but stay aware of the messages you are receiving via what you see and primarily via what you intuit. If your partner is working an honest recovery program, they will maintain open communication with you about their activities. Part of your healing as a couple means that your sex-addicted partner is now accountable to you. You may still be triggered because you've been affected by your partner's sexual acting out. Be gentle with yourself. Work your recovery. Try to discern your reactions from the reality of the situation. Of course, you *must* always ask questions and check out your perceptions with your partner.

> Perpetrators get away with their violations because their victims either stay quiet or their allegations aren't acknowledged when victims do summon the courage to speak.

"A few months after I left, Jeanne called to say that her teenage daughter had seen Kevin peering through the hedge while she and her friends were swimming in their backyard pool." What this neighbor had previously dismissed as Kevin doing yard work, she now viewed as invasive ogling that felt threatening. And she felt terrible about minimizing her daughter's earlier reported suspicions. Her reflex was to let Molly know. "This conversation was crucial for both of us," said Molly.

Molly asked Jeanne to revisit the discussion with her teenage daughter to confirm what the girl had seen and felt. So often, perpetrators get away with their violations because their victims either stay quiet or their allegations aren't acknowledged when victims do summon the courage to speak. In turn, victims begin to doubt themselves. They learn to mute and ignore their intuitions and feelings. Breaking this cycle of dismissiveness is critical.

Incidents like this regularly triggered Molly even though she no longer lived with Kevin. "Gratefully, I'd discuss these occurrences with my counselor. I learned to work through my reactions. It took me a long time to acknowledge how abused I'd been and the amount of undeserved maltreatment I'd suffered over many years. I needed to be patient with myself."

Molly was well on her way to recovery. It was clear that she could now work through her triggers and move past the feelings of worthlessness that were so familiar to her.

Some feelings of trauma have dissipated while some triggers prevail as Molly is still affected by the impact of having lived with and loved a sex addict, compounded by many years of abuse in her family of origin. "I'm hypervigilant about drawing the shades on my windows when the sun goes down," said Molly. Now, when triggered, Molly talks with people who love and support her, and she talks herself through it: "My reactions no longer run my life because they're often fear-based and fed by negative mental self-talk."

Molly's self-awareness means that she now has the power to act in her best interests, ask questions to test her perceptions, and assert her healthy boundaries when she feels triggered.

Exercise 35: What Triggers Me?

Write about what triggers your fears and insecurities.
- What triggers an emotional reaction from me?
- Do I accept less than I deserve from my intimate partner? (How does this contribute to my distress?)
- How can I deal with my triggers?

You've Tried and You Can't do This Anymore

You had decided to stay and work on your relationship together. Your partner sought help and worked on themselves. They became accountable. Active in their recovery, your partner stayed sober from sexual acting out. You worked on you. You lovingly detached from your partner, and you focused on yourself, your priorities, and your healing. You held regular check-ins with your partner. It wasn't an easy feat dealing with triggers (yours and your partner's), worrying if and when they might sexually act out again, re-establishing intimacy, and rebuilding trust—all the while focusing on your personal recovery. You had hope. You felt that the trust between you was growing. The relationship progressed, or perhaps you both coasted for some time.

Then suddenly:

Relapse

Something doesn't feel quite right. Your partner is acting secretive and distant. Your spider-sense kicks in. You feel hypervigilant, waiting for the other shoe to drop. Perhaps you're second-guessing yourself—even berating yourself for not giving your partner the benefit of the doubt, as you've quickly done before.

This time feels different, though: you're more aware, you trust your inner voice, and your tolerance threshold is lower. You want to test out your feelings because it's tearing you apart inside. It's so tough to reconcile the love you feel for your partner, along with the appealing aspects of your life together, with the possibility that they've betrayed your trust. Again.

So, you are direct when you ask your partner about their activities. At first, they dodge your queries. Then, they come up short for acceptable answers. You sense that your partner is lying, that they're covering up. Feeling shame, guilt, and self-recrimination, your partner confirms that, yes, they've returned to their sexual acting out. They've let themselves down, they've let you down, and they've jeopardized your couple relationship yet again through new episodes of intimate betrayal. The disease is stronger than them.

You feel sick with worry, fear, sadness, overwhelm, and frustration over your powerlessness to change the sex addict. Once more, you feel betrayed. Life felt sane with a semblance of normalcy (Refer to The Cycle of Sex Addiction in Chapter 1). Although you knew your partner's potential for sexually acting out, you felt secure knowing that you were doing everything you could within your couple relationship to help your partner stay sober. You were confident that they were doing their part, too.

When the sex addict relapses, this uncovers additional layers of betrayal. New and not-so-new questions arise:

- How long have these latest episodes of sexual acting out been going on?
- When did this start again? And why?
- How could I have missed the clues? (Or, I thought so, but I doubted myself!)
- What else have I missed?
- What else has the sex addict been doing/lying about?
- How did I let myself trust him/her only to experience betrayal again?
- Why won't he/she change?
- Doesn't he/she see how much this is hurting me, our relationship (and family)?

Once more, a fresh wave of reminders about your 'enoughness' comes crashing down. You are incredulous that the sex addict continues to hurt you and jeopardize your relationship. You feel like you've reached the end of your patience and tolerance. You plunge back into the stages of grieving and loss—perhaps you're all over the map feeling sad and angry, denying reality, bargaining for change, and trying to accept what is—just when you thought you'd dealt with this and had reached a resolution! Your powerlessness feels overwhelming as you face your partner's powerlessness. You've been intimately betrayed. Again! You want to understand what went wrong because you may still not comprehend the depth of your partner's disease.

Now you face a raw truth and an agonizing decision because this latest sexual acting out is your deal-breaker. You feel torn: *What if I leave and my partner does something horrible, or worse, my partner dies?* Once more, you didn't cause your partner's sexual acting out, you cannot control it, and you cannot cure it. Stronger than you is your thinking that you can still change the sex addict (Revisit Codependency in Chapter 1).

However, you cannot unknow what you now know. Let's look at the possibilities:

1. What if you leave the relationship?
2. What if you stay in the relationship?

Either way, what will your life and your relationship look like by this time next year?

Joanna's Story

Joanna's husband, Toby, began sexually acting out after staying sober for eight years. She asked to see his credit card statement on a hunch that something didn't add up in her mind. Toby reluctantly showed her the bill. The report contained numerous charges for sex chat services, and even Internet services, about which Joanna didn't know because as part of Toby's sobriety and accountability, he had no online access.

Joanna recognized the depth of Toby's disease. At the same time, she clung to the hope that they could work it out—if only Toby would go back into treatment. "Who am I kidding?" she said. "This disease is bigger than Toby." Joanna wished that this latest betrayal was not happening.

Frustrated and fearful, she faced a decision on which she couldn't turn her back: I can't do this anymore. Joanna knew that when she left Toby, she'd finally do the work she'd long put off while focused on Toby and his sex addiction. In ending the relationship, perhaps she'd open the space for Toby to hit bottom (again) and heal himself, or NOT. Joanna had no control over the outcomes, especially Toby's. Still, she loved him and wanted so much for him, perhaps more than he wanted for himself.

***

Marianne's Story

Frederic knew his potential for sexual acting out, and he relied on Marianne to keep him in check. Marianne held the passwords to their computer and ensured that parental controls remained on so that Frederic couldn't access sexual images and porn sites. Marianne spent her time and energy serving as the gatekeeper of Frederic's sexual acting out. She felt drained from being so vigilant.

But Marianne and Frederic loved each other, and so long as both were working on their respective recoveries, Marianne felt that her vigilance was crucial to their commitment. The downside was that Marianne felt that she also had to control how she sexually engaged with Frederic. She found herself avoiding sexual intimacy with Frederic because she felt unsafe to give that part of herself to Frederic while he still had the strong urge to act on his sexual compulsions. This frustrated Frederic. He wanted sexual intimacy with Marianne, but he had significant challenges separating that from the traditional porn-fueled fantasy provided by the sexual imagery that was not only in the computer but also in his head.

Then Frederic relapsed—he went out and purchased porn magazines. Marianne felt betrayed all over again. Times like this made her feel like they were back at square one. Marianne decided that she couldn't continue this way with Frederic.

***

Maureen's Story

It had been years since Maureen left her sex-addicted husband. She dated casually until finally, she met Max, an articulate, intelligent man with a great sense of humor. They shared common interests and a deep love. Maureen felt good in her relationship with Max. Then she noticed Max's hypersexuality. He'd make frequent sexual comments to Maureen about her body, often touching her out of context and in unwanted, intrusive ways. As his sex talk ramped up, Maureen felt herself withdrawing sexually. Max's behavior was proving to be a massive trigger for Maureen given her past. *Was history repeating itself?* She wondered. Maureen asserted her boundaries with Max by explaining to him how she felt he was too in her face with his constant talk about sex and that she was beginning to feel objectified. "What was glaringly clear to me this time around was my ability to identify early on what was happening in my relationship and my awareness that I would not tolerate this kind of treatment by a man," Maureen said.

***

Exercise 36: My Priorities

Reread your answers to the exercises in this book. Reflect again as you update your initial responses. You've changed. Your circumstances may also be different. What's true for you now? Record your thoughts.

What new priorities must you set for:

- Yourself?
- Your life?
- Your continued healing?

Exercise 37: What Would I do If...?

1. What would you do if you have decided to stay with your beloved partner and then you discovered that they've relapsed into sexual acting out and intimate betrayal?

If this is not your reality, try on another perspective:

2. If you've left, knowing what you now know, what would you do if you discovered that your new partner was sexually acting out?

Note: the goal is not to breed or feed fear, but rather, to invite you to think about your boundaries and how you'd enact these 'If.' When we plan for adversity, we can be proactive in prioritizing and taking care of ourselves.

Remember that your foundation has been shaken — if not shattered. You can rebuild a new foundation based on your strengths and self-love and by putting yourself and your life first.

You can do this!

Chapter 8

Embracing the Gains

Losing something in one aspect of your life often results in gaining something else—even if it isn't apparent right away. These are the countless gifts you didn't have before or during the deception and chaos. These gains can include:

- Serenity
- Peace of mind
- Feeling less burdened by guilt
- Happiness/joy/freedom
- Deeper friendships
- Self-worth
- More time for yourself and your priorities
- Clear, healthy boundaries
- Assertiveness

- Trust
- Compassion
- (List any others here.)

Exercise 38: My Gratitude Journal

Each day, in your journal, write five to ten things in your life for which you are grateful and the reasons you are thankful. Do this every day—and watch the good things that life offers flowing to and around you!

Here are some examples:

- Right now, I'm grateful for the company of my dog whose presence is calming for me.
- Today I feel grateful for the visit with my brother and his family because they made me laugh. I feel good being with them.
- I feel grateful for my career, which provides meaning, financial stability, and security.
- I am grateful for the warm sun today because it feels good on my skin.

Appreciate all that you have. Abundance flows when you recognize even the smallest things!

Cultivating Self-Love and Self-Worthiness

Displacement or loss of self, self-love, and self-worthiness can be massive when healing from intimate betrayal. Slowly, you are learning to love and prioritize yourself again. You may have put the needs of the sex addict far above your own while keeping a lid on the chaos surrounding their sexual acting out. Helping an addict who will not help themselves is a bottomless pit. You cannot fill their void. You can't do for the sex addict what they cannot do for themselves.

> **“** Self-love is how you prioritize yourself and your needs as an expression of your self-worthiness in the face of others' demands and expectations.

Because you are a caring, loving, and intelligent person, you want to help others. Giving is an admirable quality. Now you must learn to apply this nurturing to help yourself. This process takes time. It's a daily practice of love.

Molly explained how she was a giver in her relationship: "I would often be the one to make concessions, apologize, and smooth things over. I was forever trying to make the relationship work with Kevin, despite how hopeless the circumstances. I'd suck it up. I was patient to a fault. I was loyal. I was too tolerant of Kevin's unacceptable behavior. It dawned on me that Kevin was a taker. He was too willing to foist the responsibility for the well-being of our relationship onto me, a task I was quick to assume because I'm a giver. When I finally put all that effort and energy into loving myself and letting myself feel worthy, I had more space, both mentally and physically."

Self-love is about more than taking a bubble bath, turning off the phone, or going to bed early. Loving yourself is how you take care of and prioritize your own needs in relationship with others. It is how you honor and exercise your healthy boundaries. Self-love is how you prioritize yourself and your needs as an expression of your self-worthiness in the face of others' demands and expectations.

Self-Love and Celibacy

Loving yourself is also about how you express your sexuality—with yourself and with another. Betrayal by the person with whom you are intimate and share your sexuality can profoundly affect your view of yourself as a sexual being, along with your trust in both yourself and others regarding sex.

It may now feel unsafe for you sexually. If you stay, you may worry about your partner's sexual sobriety. If you leave, you may worry about encountering another relationship with a sex addict. Whether you go or stay, you may fear that you're not attractive or sexy enough should you choose to engage sexually again. You may experience a variety of reactions—from hypersexuality (perhaps based on a heightened need for self-validation and sexual reassurance) to complete abstinence.

When you experience intimate betrayal, you may question your whole self-concept. You might wonder: *Am I sexy enough?* This question goes beyond the physical aspect of your sexuality. It may reach deep into your inner core, where the intimate betrayal has hit hardest. Your partner's sexual deviance/sex addiction doesn't define your sexuality, your value, or your self-worth.

You can retrieve your sexual esteem. How might that look? For some, this might be engaging with another sexual partner right away, which could result in a rebound relationship with its own set of issues. For others, it might mean taking a break from sex with another person or with your partner (if you have decided to stay).

Celibacy—abstaining from sexual relations with another person for a significant period—is, for some, an ugly word. After all, we are sexual beings seeking relationship and connection. Why would anyone want to practice celibacy?

Consider abstaining from sex with your partner/another person through conscious and planned celibacy as you establish a healthy boundary for yourself. Choosing this path means delaying/postponing sexual intimacy with a partner for the time being.

Celibacy can benefit you because it can help you:

- Achieve clarity about your relationship
- Get clear about what gives your life meaning
- Become more objective about your needs, wants, likes, and dislikes
- Make yourself a priority
- Set goals for your own life and future
- Make decisions in your own best interests
- Heal in your self-love, self-image, and self-respect

Most importantly, don't feel pressured by your partner to re-engage sexually. Be firm in your resolve, and lovingly detach from any need for validation. If you've decided to stay, there are other ways to cultivate intimacy that do not involve sex—for the time being. Remember, you must rebuild trust.

"When I first discovered Kevin's sexual acting out, I immediately moved into my home office," recalls Molly. "I decided to no longer have sex with Kevin—despite the pressure he exerted in attempting to bargain with me for it. He even offered to fix my car if I'd have sex with him!"

Why the conscious and planned celibacy? First, Molly was turned off: "I felt disgusted. I had to honor my disinterest, let it sink in, and deal with it. Secondly, I knew that re-engaging sexually with Kevin meant, for me, re-engaging emotionally." Such re-bonding risked muddying Molly's perceptions: "I felt vulnerable. I didn't want to risk Kevin manipulating me into staying in this dysfunctional dynamic. I didn't want to revert to my old refrain: Things will get better if only …"

The bottom line was that by not re-engaging sexually, Molly was expressing a healthy boundary. Foundational for setting future limits, celibacy helped Molly get her needs met as she prioritized herself and her life.

"By detaching from Kevin in all ways, I began to see through the haze of the chaos. I started to make clear decisions about my next steps—about my choice to end our relationship." Molly was tempted to give in, but she would not let Kevin persuade her with more empty promises that things would change. In fact, by sitting back and observing, Molly watched Kevin's behavior deteriorate further. Now he was openly antagonistic toward her, slinging angry barbs. "The situation worsened." Molly's detached observations affirmed her decision. "This validated my choice not to re-engage sexually or emotionally, and ultimately, that I had made the right decision."

Celibacy also served Molly well when she began dating. "I decided I wouldn't share something precious to me before seeing whether a relationship had merit." She'd read about the importance of postponing sexual intimacy until a healthy relationship is well-established: "I was able to express my self-respect and self-worth and then make a clear decision about a relationship."

Jenn's Story

When Jenn discovered that her partner, Jeremy, was a sex addict, she immediately gave him an ultimatum: "Get help or get out."

Jeremy was hitting bottom. He valued his five-year relationship with Jenn and wanted to work things out together.

They each sought professional help and joined support groups.

Jenn decided to suspend having sexual relations with Jeremy. Trust needed rebuilding. For his part, Jeremy had to relearn how to be intimate with Jenn in ways that didn't involve sex.

It was going on two years of abstinence, and both were working diligently in their respective recovery programs despite the many challenges and ever-present triggers.

Jenn said, "I have no clue what the future holds for us and our relationship. I'll wait and see. For now, I love Jeremy, and we're committed to making our relationship healthy."

***

When we engage sexually with another person, we risk losing our self-focus, especially if we feel captivated, usually in the early stages of a new relationship when we tend to experience infatuation involving intense feelings of euphoria. Marking this phase is a surge in hormones, such as endorphins, which lead to heightened serotonin levels. We feel happier—like we're walking on clouds—and we have difficulty focusing on our life, our work, and our other relationships. We can't stop thinking about the other person and we feel excited at the possibility of seeing them again and of sexual contact. During this phase, we experience the glow of being in love. Being in this state affects our perception of the other person, the relationship, and our true feelings.

We need to take time before diving into sex at this stage so the fog can clear, and we can make healthy decisions based on our values. For this reason, it's always best to wait three to six months before engaging sexually with another person. Once we overcome the initial infatuation, we can see the real person and the dynamic between us so that we can be clear about whether this relationship serves us and our needs and wants. We also have the opportunity to set our worth at this point. Immediately or prematurely falling into bed with a new person or with our recovering sex-addicted partner risks sending the message that we have porous boundaries and low self-esteem.

Waiting before engaging sexually also enables us to see if this is the kind of relationship we want to have. If someone is abusive toward us, having had sex too early may have forged an emotional bond that makes us feel hesitant to end the relationship. It feels complicated to let go when there are some redeeming aspects of the relationship. In other words, we've already invested.

Postponing sex with another person allows us to work on developing the emotional bond and mutual respect necessary for true intimacy. It enables us to get to know each other and build trust and friendship. Sex is but one activity; there are so many ways to engage with another person that can foster a stable, healthy relationship.

Consider not even embarking on a new relationship while you're trying to heal. As already mentioned, new love relationships tend to distract us with those intense feelings of infatuation inherently produced by endorphins, which can affect our clear-headed thinking and decision-making. By dedicating ourselves to the vital work of healing from intimate betrayal, we can avoid rebounding, finding someone else to rescue, or making relationship choices that go against our values. We can take the time to get to know our wants and needs so that we can readily convey these and have them met in a future healthy, reciprocal relationship.

You can channel your sexual energy into activities (See Holistic Healing Activities and Practices in Chapter 5) aimed at getting to know yourself and what you like, need, and want. Ultimately, by channeling your sexual energy into focusing on yourself, you'll regain your sense of self-worthiness, which will help you to heal.

"I recall a coffee date with someone I'd met through an Internet dating site. He told me that he'd been separated from his wife for three months, but that they were still living together. They had two young children. When I asked him about his plans to move out, he said something about possibly staying with a friend. I wasn't interested in someone who had yet to figure out the logistics of his new life. I was almost four years into my recovery at that point. That meeting was our first and last." Molly said.

Life had presented Molly with another test, an opportunity to see how far she'd come in her journey. She wasn't getting involved with someone who still hadn't finalized their current relationship status because it would only complicate her life (See Life Tests in Chapter 6).

Exercise 39: Prioritizing and Getting My Needs Met

What are my primary needs? Write five to ten needs that you have and the specific ways you will choose to get these needs met.

Exercise 40: My Plan for Sexual Self-Expression

How I will manage my sexual self-expression?

In our quest for love and belonging, we all want to be seen by others. We yearn for this to feel connected. We especially wish for a lover to see and witness us. You can give this gift to yourself by expressing self-love. This next exercise facilitates this practice.

Exercise 41: Writing a Love Letter to Myself

You will need a hand mirror for this exercise. Think of all those qualities and characteristics that you'd like to hear a lover say they love and appreciate about you. You may want to revisit the Mirror Mirror exercise and the I AM exercise in Chapter 5.

1. Hold your mirror up comfortably to your face. Without judgment, see yourself.

2. Looking into your own eyes, tell yourself aloud what you like, love, and appreciate about yourself. Continue to see yourself. Witness YOU.

3. Now, put the mirror aside and write a love letter to yourself, detailing all the things that you love about yourself. Express your love and appreciation for all the physical, emotional, and spiritual aspects of your whole being. Don't censor yourself.

4. Read your love letter aloud to yourself. Then put it away in a safe place.

5. Revisit, reread, and revise your love letter from time to time. Or, you might seal your love letter in an envelope, date it, then open it much later (one year from writing).

As you begin to restore the fractured pieces of your life after an intimate betrayal, rather than focusing on the losses, you'll come to realize and appreciate your progress. As you recognize and embrace your hard-won gains, you'll learn to protect and nurture them. There will be no going back to unhealthy patterns — not without being consciously aware. Again, you cannot unknow what you now know.

Chapter 9

Rewrite Your Story

There *is* life after intimate betrayal—*your life*. You can write the next chapter of your story, one that includes health and well-being as you prioritize yourself and your needs. You'll expand into your 'enoughness' and continue to grow in your feelings of self-worth.

Let's visualize what that looks like by creating a snapshot of the life you want to embrace and enjoy.

Here's your parting homework: create a vision board. A vision board is a tool to help you visualize and build your future full of positive outcomes. A vision board is a visual representation using words, phrases, and pictures of that which you desire and value. First, you must believe you can have what you want. You put the intention out there. Then you can attract it!

> **EXERCISE 42: VISIONING THE NEXT CHAPTER OF MY STORY**

Apply these steps to create your very own vision board:

1. Buy a large firm poster board from an office supply or dollar store.
2. Clip inspiring positive pictures, words, phrases, and quotes from discarded magazines, newspapers, and the Internet.
3. Attach these to your board with a glue stick, tape, or tacks.
4. Keep returning to this activity over time, filling your board.

Creating a vision board is an energy-changing activity; it is not a panacea. Avoid obsessing over your vision board because this is not a magic wand that will make everything better or make all your dreams suddenly materialize. The goal is to live your life with intention. When we live with intention, we focus on what is vital and meaningful for us. We honor and champion our values. We clarify our needs. We dare to want. We prioritize our life.

Display your board in a strategic place where your subconscious mind can absorb the visuals. Take time every day to look at what you've posted. Notice what you now attract. Revisit the gratitude exercise in Chapter 7. Be grateful for each new positive experience, person, and learning. You'll see how, over time, the miracles begin to unfold in your life.

Takeaway

Humans have incredible resiliency. We have the power to grow from the most tragic of circumstances. We learn from the tough stuff.

Molly stood back from her vision board and said, "My most significant learning is that I *am* enough. I am more than my earliest stories. I am not my feelings. And I can transcend my feelings about my story."

From her inauspicious beginnings living in an unfinished home rife with violence and addiction—an unsafe home perpetually under construction and renovation—to moving in with yet another abusive addict and unsuccessfully trying to fix all the wrongs of her legacy, Molly has reconstructed her life. She no longer feels alone trying to hold up the T-bar support because she unsuspectingly partnered with someone unable to give her any more than her father could. "I accepted so little because I was unaware of my deservingness. I know that I deserve much more. Now I have the power to give that to myself." Molly no longer negotiates her self-worth with other people.

> My scar is a badge of honor on my hero's journey.

Today, Molly is not a betrayed victim. She has peeled off the labels. Once lifted, they left a scar that reminded Molly of her vulnerability and resiliency. Molly now declares triumphantly, "My scar is a badge of honor on my hero's journey!"

You know how awful it felt to walk through the fire of your discovery. You know the searing pain of its aftermath. You've taken bold steps to the other side. What joy and beauty reside there? Do you want it now? You are worthy of enjoying the gifts life offers as you create and attract:

- Clarity
- Joy
- Health and well-being

- Support
- Beauty
- Love
- Peace and serenity
- Abundance
- And more (Make a list)!

Think back to the start of your journey and where you are now. What is *your* takeaway?

Exercise 43: What I've Learned that's Worth Remembering

1. What have I learned about myself through my transition?
2. How can I leverage what I've learned to move forward with my life?

You are attracting only favorable, healthy situations and relationships into your life. You deserve to be happy and fulfilled. And now you not only know that you are enough—you *feel* that you are enough.

Let's say it together out loud: I AM ENOUGH.

Epilogue

Often, we're looking for that happy ending. I think that's why fairy tales are so enchanting. They offer up a shiny package tied with a happily-ever-after bow. We want that! And we can create it for ourselves on our terms. We can add rich layers that texture our narratives as we empower ourselves to script new chapters of our story.

Molly was once where you may find yourself now: lost in bleak darkness and suffering an intimate partner's betrayal. Molly was bound to the legacy of a dysfunctional life through her notions of self-blame and fear. She had so much work ahead to pull herself out of the abyss. Molly made the tough decision to end her couple relationship so she could heal. She had to leave and grieve the loss of all she'd known.

We witnessed Molly stepping out of the darkness. We watched her blossom through the uncertainties of creating a new life from the ashes of despair as she walked through the fire to get to the other side. We saw Molly redefine herself as separate from those grim chapters of her story.

Molly began the process of prioritizing her life, one that involved years of healing on all levels. She was on a mission to reclaim her sense of self. She felt whole as she prioritized her needs, wants, values, and life. Molly worked hard for her recovery.

Today, Molly is the architect of her own finished house with smooth floors upon which her feet stand firmly. She walks safely. "I'm secure in my core as I proclaim the words: 'I am enough.' Life throws me lemons from time to time, but I know that I possess the inner resources to overcome these challenges. I squeeze the hell out of them, and I make lemonade!"

 We can hoard our stories and feel shame—or we can share our narratives in all their rawness and break free of their bonds.

Molly broke the pattern of victimhood. She stopped settling for less than she deserved. Molly started to love herself enough and unconditionally. "I felt whole and complete on my own. I realized that I'd always been enough exactly as I am."

***

When I first sat down to write this book, I never thought it would take on a life of its own—one that would put me in the service of others, accompanying them along their journeys by sharing composites of their experiences with intimate betrayal.

In the film, *Seeing Allred* (2018), Gloria Steinem says, "The final stage of healing is using what happened to you to help other people. That is the healing in itself."

In telling these stories, I've underscored my insights into the human experience of intimate betrayal. I've learned that we can hoard our stories and feel shame—or we can share our narratives in all their rawness and break free of their bonds.

I have written *I AM ENOUGH* to help us all break free.

Releasing this book is my most prominent act of vulnerability and faith yet. *I AM ENOUGH* sails into the world now, no longer mine. Instead, it joins a brave collective who use it to heal.

You've taken the bold step of facing the most difficult challenge: a significant life transition. Alongside Molly, you've told your own story as you've worked through the various chapters designed to shed light on your narrative. You've courageously explored, questioned, and reflected. Perhaps you've learned that being enough is so much more than you ever dreamed.

Recently I was asked how you learn to trust someone else after you've experienced betrayal in your intimate relationship. The short answer is: you learn to trust yourself.

In the wise words of Nora Ephron: "Above all, be the heroine of your life, not the victim."

Go forward in peace and serenity on your journey. May you continue to grow in your self-love and self-worthiness. You *are* enough!

Recommended Resources

Books

Courage to Change: One Day at a Time in Al-Anon II, Al-Anon Family Group Headquarters, Inc. (1992).

Codependent No More: How to Stop Controlling Others and Start Caring for Yourself. Melody Beattie (2006).

Breaking the Cycle of Abuse: How to Move Beyond Your Past to Create an Abuse-Free Future. Beverly Engel, LMFT (2005).

Don't Call It Love: Recovery from Sexual Addiction, Dr. Patrick Carnes, PhD (1991).

In the Realm of Hungry Ghosts: Close Encounters with Addiction, Dr. Gabor Mate (2009).

Mending a Shattered Heart: A Guide for Partners of Sex Addicts, Stefanie Carnes, PhD (2011).

The Language of Letting Go, Melody Beattie (1990).

The Emotionally Abusive Relationship: How to Stop Being Abused and How to Stop Abusing, Beverly Engel, LMFT (2003).

The Porn Trap: The Essential Guide to Overcoming Problems Caused by Pornography, Wendy Maltz and Larry Maltz (2010).

Your Sexually Addicted Spouse: How Partners Can Cope and Heal, Barbara Steffens, PhD, and Marsha Means, MA (2009).

Websites

Dayton, Tian, PhD. *Intimacy in Recovery*: http://fullspectrumrecovery.com/wp-content/uploads/2013/06/Intimacy-in-Recovery.pdf
Joe Polish's interview with Dr. Patrick Carnes, PhD, leading sex addiction expert: www.youtube.com/watch?v=m7TwURjJo80 (2015)

Married to a Sex Addict: www.marriedtoasexaddict.com

Mate, Gabor, PhD (2018). *The Hungry Ghost Inside Us*. Sustainable Human video: www.facebook.com/SustainableMan/videos/10155327895662909/?hc_ref=ARQvSPrHZy7iHAehH-tO99znmSyIKH9zrRYM_x4JKf4nbfG_ZLrepu39qpC4HRJrBIO-w&pnref=story

Sex Addicts Anonymous (SAA) - support for sex addicts: www.saa-recovery.org/

S-Anon International Family Groups - support for family and friends of sex addicts: www.sanon.org

Sexaholics Anonymous (SA) - support for people with problems of lust, sex, and pornography addiction: www.sa.org/

Sex Help: www.sexhelp.com
SOS Sisterhood of Support: www.sisterhoodofsupport.org

Bibliography

Al-Anon Family Group Headquarters Inc. 1992. "The Three C's of Al-Anon" in *Courage to Change: One Day at a Time in Al-Anon II*, p. 74.

Allely, Sarah. March 27, 2018. *His Other Life*, SBS: www.sbs.com.au/news/insight/tvepisode/his-other-life

American Psychiatric Association. *What is Depression?* www.psychiatry.org/patients-families/depression/what-is-depression

American Psychiatric Association. 2013. *Diagnostic and Statistical Manual of Mental Disorders* (5th ed.). Arlington, VA: American Psychiatric Publishing.

Bergland, Christopher. 2016. "The Neuroscience of Fear and Post-Traumatic Stress." *Psychology Today*: www.psychologytoday.com/blog/the-athletes-way/201601/the-neuroscience-fear-responses-and-post-traumatic-stress

Brown, Brené, PhD. 2019. *Braving the Wilderness: The Quest for True Belonging and the Courage to Stand Alone*. New York: Random House.

Brown, Brené, PhD. 2012. *Daring Greatly: How the Courage to be Vulnerable Transforms the Way We Live, Love, Parent, and Lead.* New York: Gotham Books.

Brownstein, Bill. May 31, 2018. "Montreal CEO of adult site says #MeToo counts in her world, too," *Montreal Gazette*.

Campbell, Joseph, and Kudler, David. 2008. *Pathways to Bliss: Mythology and Personal Transformation.* Sydney: ReadHowYouWant.

Carnes, Patrick, PhD. *Cycle of Addiction.* (Edited by Marnie Ferree, MA, LMFT, CSAT and Laura M. Brotherson, MS, MFT). October 2013.

Carnes, Patrick, PhD. 2011. Video interview with Joe Polish's Genius Network: www.youtube.com/watch?v=i1pQfGD_MQI.

Chapman, Tracy, co-produced with Tchad Blake. 2005. "Change" from *Where You Live*. Label: Elektra.

Cowan, Eleanor. 2013. *A History of a Pedophile's Wife: Memoir of a Canadian Teacher and Writer.* BookBaby Publishers.

Cruchet, Dawn. May 29, 2013. Community Health and Social Services Network Community Health Education Program (CHEP) video conference presentation, "Demystifying Grief," Montreal, Quebec.

Daily Mail. 2011. "'I thought I'd never sing again.': Shania Twain reveals how heartbreak of husband leaving her for best friend took its toll on her voice." www.dailymail.co.uk/tvshowbiz/article-1383330/Shania-Twain-reveals-divorce-heartbreak-husbands-affair-friend-Oprah.html

Engel, Beverly. 2002. *The Emotionally Abusive Relationship: How to Stop Being Abused and How to Stop Abusing*, New Jersey: John Wiley & Sons, Inc.

Ephron, Nora. February 2018: www.goodreads.com/quotes/tag/courage

Gray, John, PhD. 2001. *Mars and Venus in the Bedroom: A Guide to Lasting Romance and Passion*. HarperTorch Publishers.

Haanel, Charles F. 1916 (Reprinted in 2017). *The Master Key System*. Digireads.com Publishing.

Kelley, Anita E., PhD. November 10, 2010. "Are People Who Act Superior Really Insecure?" *Psychology Today*: www.psychologytoday.com/ca/blog/insight/201011/are-people-who-act-superior-really-insecure

Kübler-Ross, Elisabeth. 2014. *On Death and Dying: What the Dying Have to Teach Doctors, Nurses, Clergy and Their Own Families* (Reissue edition). Scribner.

Lee, Chris. November 25, 2011. "The Sex Addiction Epidemic," *Newsweek*: www.newsweek.com/sex-addiction-epidemic-66289

Lloyd, Alexander, PhD. 2018. "Cellular Memory Healing: How to Clear Limiting Beliefs and Memories at the Cellular Level," *Conscious Lifestyle*: www.consciouslifestylemag.com/cellular-memory-healing-clearing/

Mate, Gabor, PhD. 2018. *The Hungry Ghost Inside Us*. Sustainable Human video: www.facebook.com/SustainableMan/videos/10155327895662909/?hcref=ARQvSPrHZy7iHAehH-tO99znmSyIKH9zrRYM_x4JKf4nbfG_ZLrepu39qpC4I IRJıBIO-w&pnref=story

Marie Forleo's interview with Dr. Brené Brown, PhD. September 12, 2017. *Brené Brown Shows You How to "Brave the Wilderness."* MarieTV online: www.youtube.com/watch?v=A9FopgKyAfI

Mayo Clinic. 2018. *Post-traumatic Stress Disorder (PTSD):* www.mayoclinic.org/diseases-conditions/post-traumatic-stress-disorder/symptoms-causes/syc-20355967

Moran, Robert A., PhD. July 3, 2018. *Are Addicts Sociopaths?* LoveFraud: www.lovefraud.com/are-addicts-sociopaths/

Rogers, Barb. 2011. "Sex Addiction: Explanation or Excuse? Five Common Traits," *Huffington Post*: www.huffingtonpost.com/barb-rogers/sex-addiction-explanation_b_539606.html.

SAnon International Family Groups, Inc.: www.sanon.org

Steinem, Gloria. 2018. *Seeing Allred.* Netflix Original film.

Stosny, Steven, PhD. July 13, 2013. "Types of Intimate Betrayal," *Psychology Today*: www.psychologytoday.com/us/blog/anger-in-the-age-entitlement/201307/types-intimate-betrayal

The Ranch. 2018. *Sex Addiction in America: Is it Common?*: www.recoveryranch.com/resources/sex-addiction-and-intimacy-disorders/sex-addiction-america-common/

Tolle, Eckhart. 2003. *Stillness Speaks.* London: Hodder & Stoughton Publishers.

Twain, Shania. 2011. *From This Moment On.* New York: Simon & Schuster, Inc.

Walker, Lenore E., PhD. 1980. *The Battered Woman* (Fourth Edition). William Morrow Paperbacks.

Zacchia, Camillo, PhD. October 19, 2016. In conversation in Montreal, Quebec.

www.ingramcontent.com/pod-product-compliance
Lightning Source LLC
Chambersburg PA
CBHW081409080526

44589CB00016B/2509